AZUMANGA DAIOH
THE MANGA
1

Creator **Kiyohiko Azuma**

あずまきよひこ

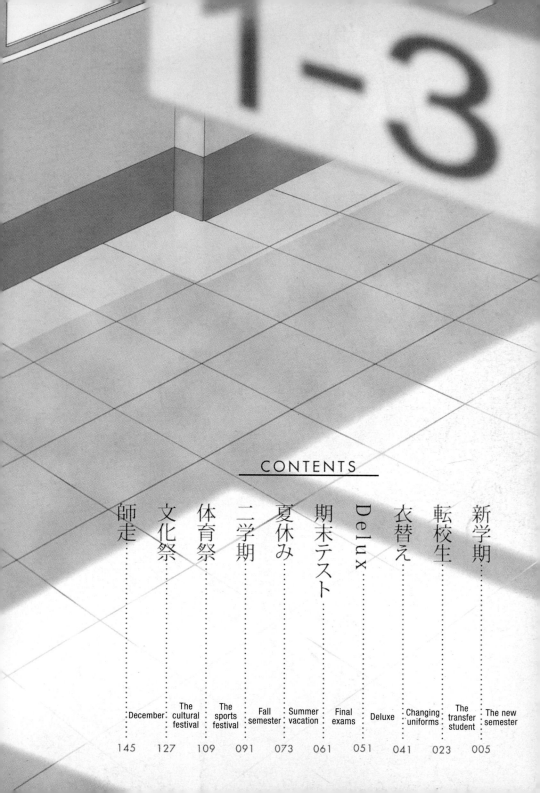

CONTENTS

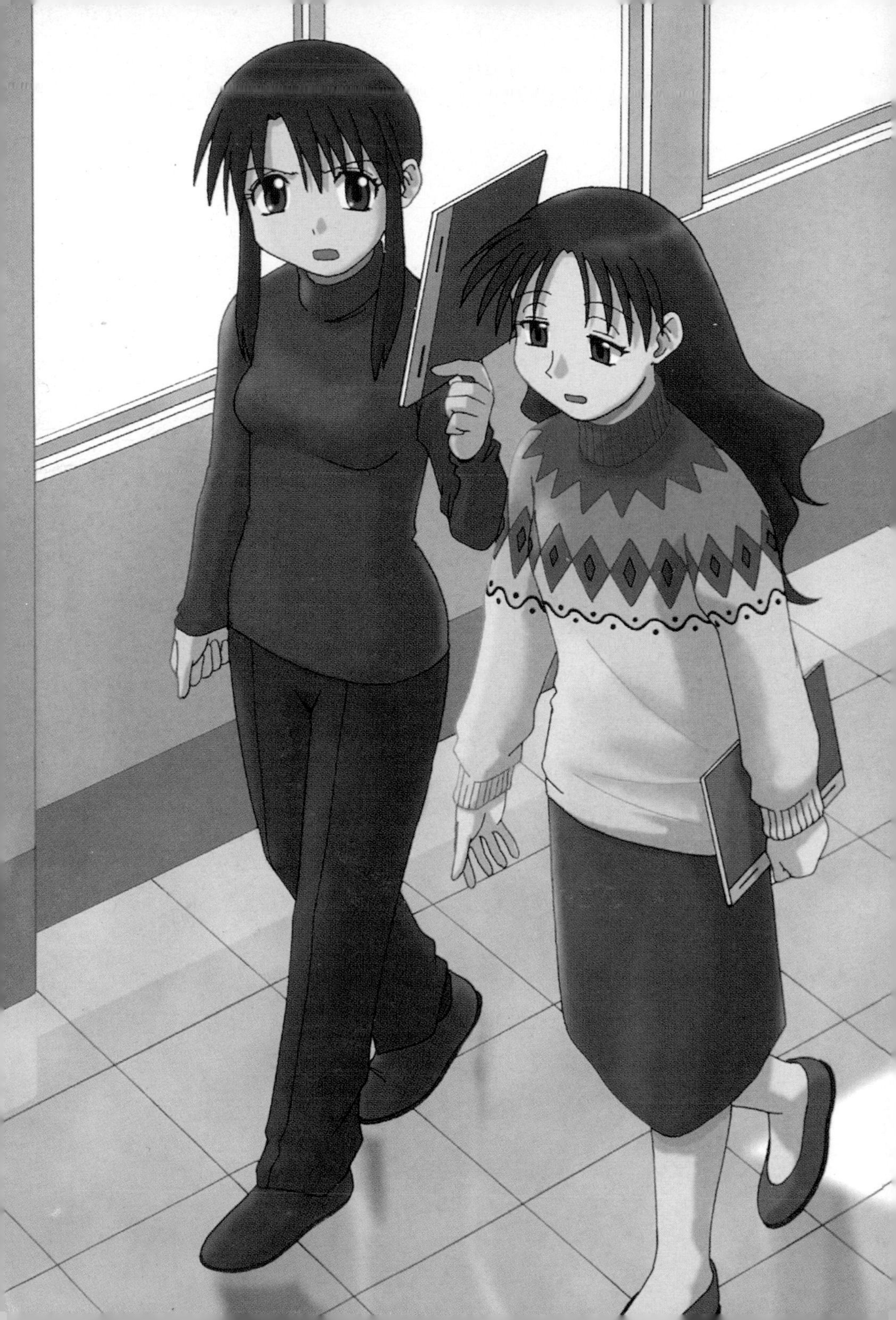

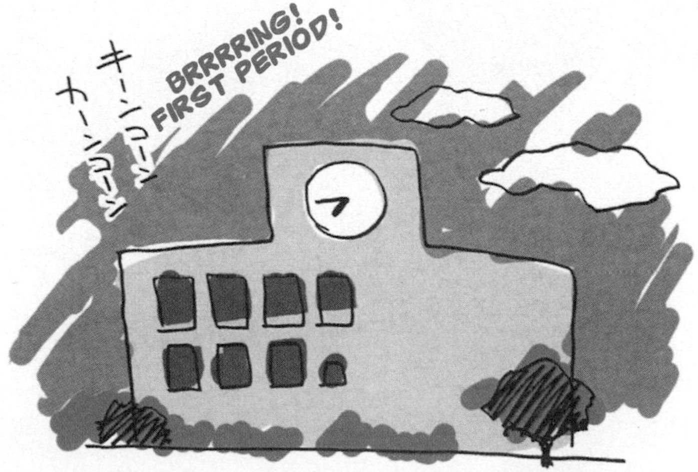
キーンコーン
カーンコーン
BRRRRING!
FIRST PERIOD!

MISS YUKARI

4 APRIL PART-1

AZU MANGA DAIOH

MA'AM?

YUKARI TANIZAKI

HELLO, EVERYBODY! I'M MISS TANIZAKI, HAPPY TO BE HERE IN ROOM 3! IF YOU HAVE ANY QUESTIONS, JUST ASK!

NO! YOU CANNOT ASK MY BRA SIZE!

UM, MISS YU-KARI...?

I DON'T MEAN TO BRAG, BUT...

AND IT'S **NOT** 'CUZ I'M EMBARRASSED.

WELL, UH... YOUR CLASS IS NEXT DOOR. THIS IS ROOM 4.

WHY AM I TELLING YOU THIS? ANYWAY, WHAT WAS YOUR QUESTION?

I ALWAYS HATE THE FIRST DAY BACK...

POP QUIZ 1

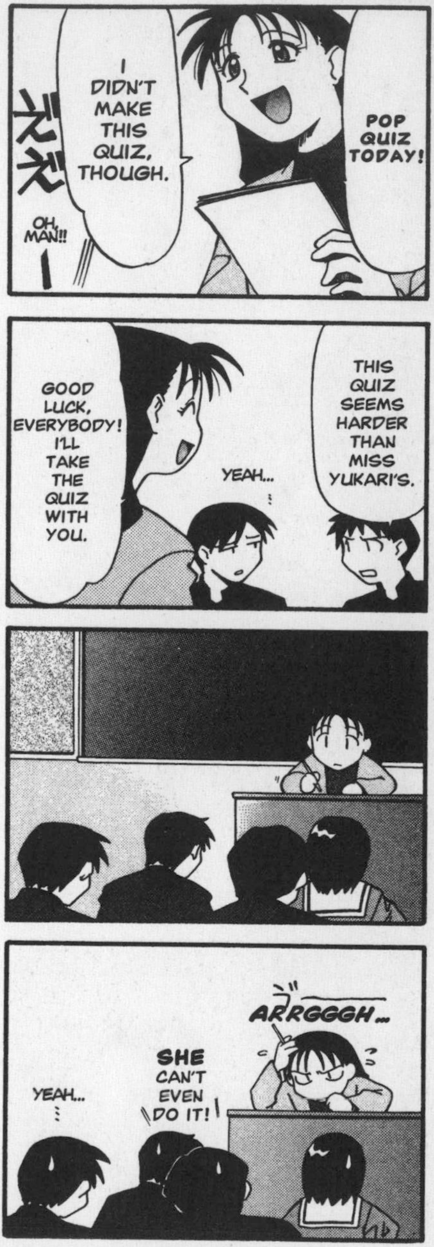

POP QUIZ TODAY!
I DIDN'T MAKE THIS QUIZ, THOUGH.
ええ
OH, MAN!!
THIS QUIZ SEEMS HARDER THAN MISS YUKARI'S.
YEAH...
GOOD LUCK, EVERYBODY! I'LL TAKE THE QUIZ WITH YOU.
ARRGGGH...
SHE CAN'T EVEN DO IT!
YEAH...

POP QUIZ 2

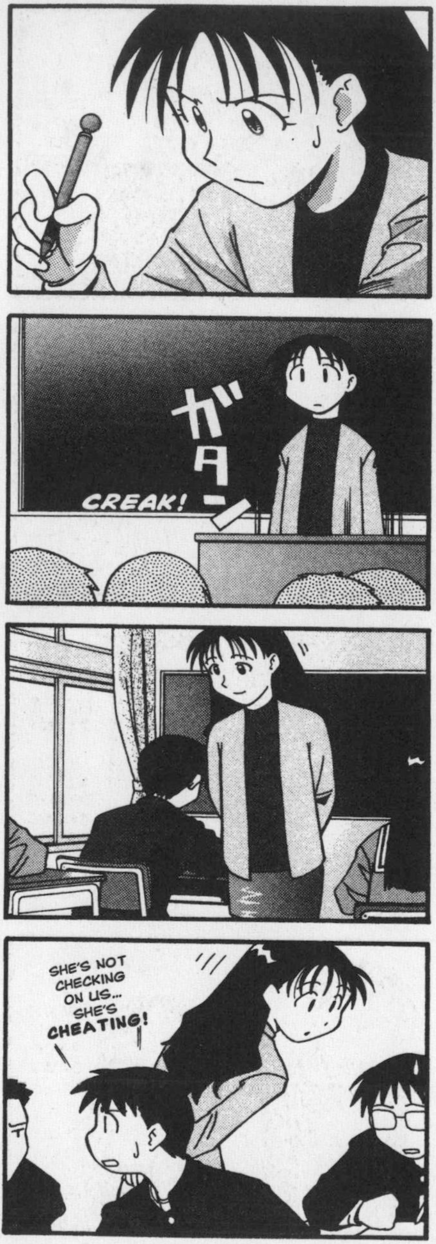

ガタ
CREAK!
SHE'S NOT CHECKING ON US... SHE'S CHEATING!

CHILD PRODIGY

DON'T GET COCKY!

PERFECT

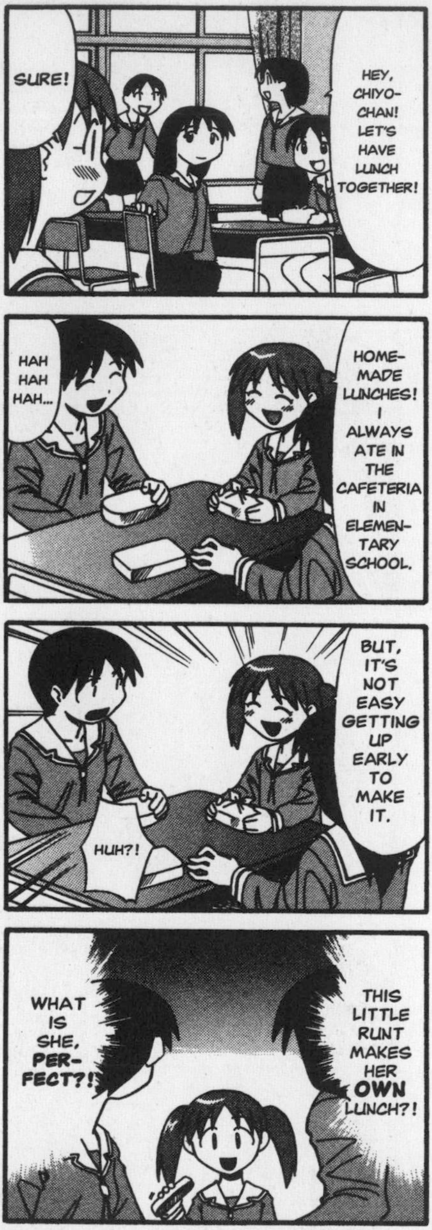
HEY, CHIYO-CHAN! LET'S HAVE LUNCH TOGETHER!
SURE!
HOME-MADE LUNCHES! I ALWAYS ATE IN THE CAFETERIA IN ELEMENTARY SCHOOL.
HAH HAH HAH...
BUT, IT'S NOT EASY GETTING UP EARLY TO MAKE IT.
HUH?!
THIS LITTLE RUNT MAKES HER OWN LUNCH?!
WHAT IS SHE, PERFECT?!

GENIUS

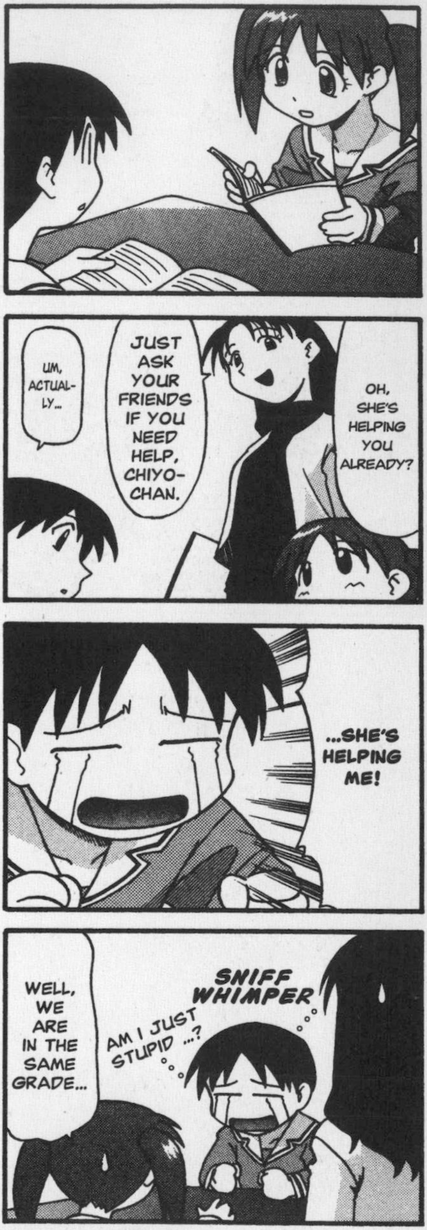
JUST ASK YOUR FRIENDS IF YOU NEED HELP, CHIYO-CHAN.
UM, ACTUALLY...
OH, SHE'S HELPING YOU ALREADY?
...SHE'S HELPING ME!
WELL, WE ARE IN THE SAME GRADE...
SNIFF WHIMPER
AM I JUST STUPID ...?

SAKAKI'S COOL   SCARY?

WHISPER WHISPER

SHE LOOKS KINDA SCARY, BUT COOLER THAN THE GUYS.

DON'T YOU THINK SAKAKI'S COOL?

WHISPER WHISPER

DAILY HELPER

OH, I GOTTA GET EVERY-ONE'S PAPERS.

SHE'S COOL... AND SHE'S COLD, TOO!

HI ...CAN I GET YOUR LIST?

にゃーん

MEEEE-YOOW!

HERE!

UM...

SHE LOOKS SCARY...

ARE THOSE KITTY PANTIES I JUST SAW?!

HEY, SHE MIGHT BE NICE...

CAREER CHOICES
· VETERINARIAN
· FLORIST
· SALES PERSON AT A TOYSTORE

ALONE

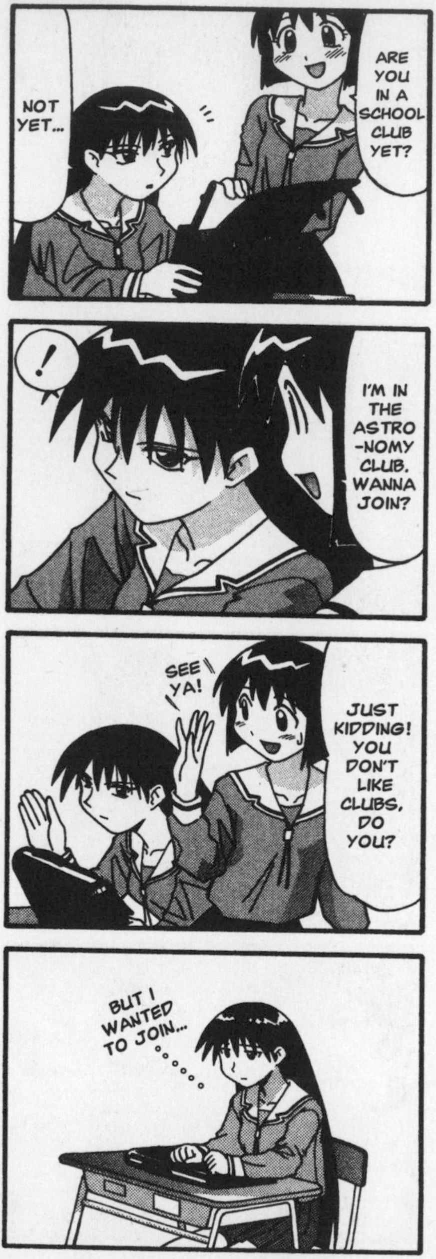
ARE YOU IN A SCHOOL CLUB YET?
NOT YET...
!
I'M IN THE ASTRO-NOMY CLUB. WANNA JOIN?
JUST KIDDING! YOU DON'T LIKE CLUBS, DO YOU?
SEE YA!
BUT I WANTED TO JOIN...

KITTY CAT...

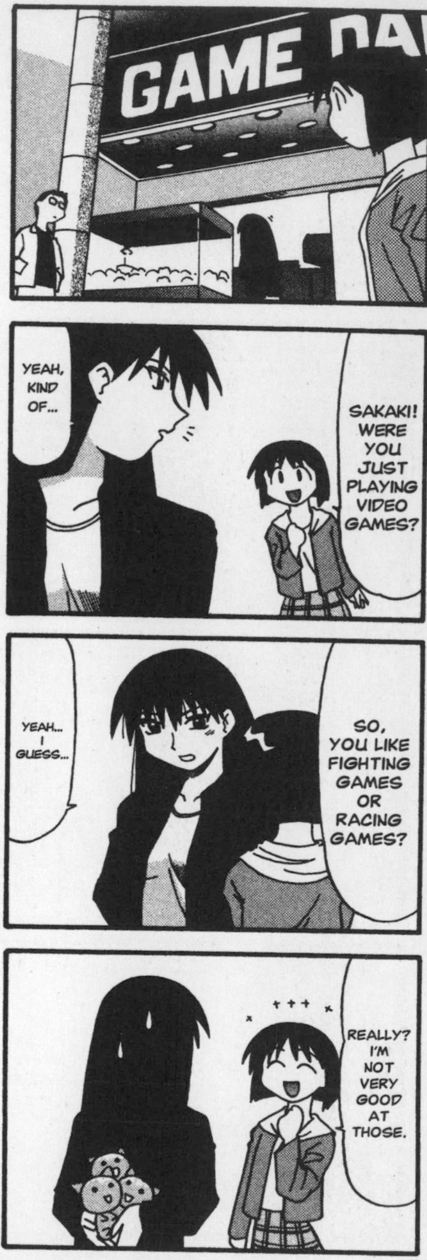
GAME
SAKAKI! WERE YOU JUST PLAYING VIDEO GAMES?
YEAH, KIND OF...
SO, YOU LIKE FIGHTING GAMES OR RACING GAMES?
YEAH... I GUESS...
REALLY? I'M NOT VERY GOOD AT THOSE.

TOMO DON'T GIVE UP!

WHAT?! YOU DON'T REALLY HAVE TO...

EXCUSE ME! FORGOT MY HOMEWORK! I'M READY FOR MY PUNISHMENT NOW.

HEH HEH... I'VE ALWAYS WANTED TO DO THIS, JUST ONCE!

MAN! SO HEAVY!

SHE'S SO ANNOYING...

HEY! A FLOOD! TEACHER...!

OH NO! I DROPPED THEM!

CRASH! SLOSH SLOSH

TOMO GONE WILD!

I'VE GOT MORE ENERGY THAN ANYONE!

I'M TOMO TAKINO.

OK! YOU, TOMO!

PICK ME!

SOMEBODY PLEASE READ THIS PAGE.

SWOOSH

"ME LLAMO <SU NOMBRE>, COMO TE LLAMAS?"

I REMEMBER THAT BOOK!

WHOOPS! I BROUGHT MY 7TH GRADE BOOK!

RUN TOMO!

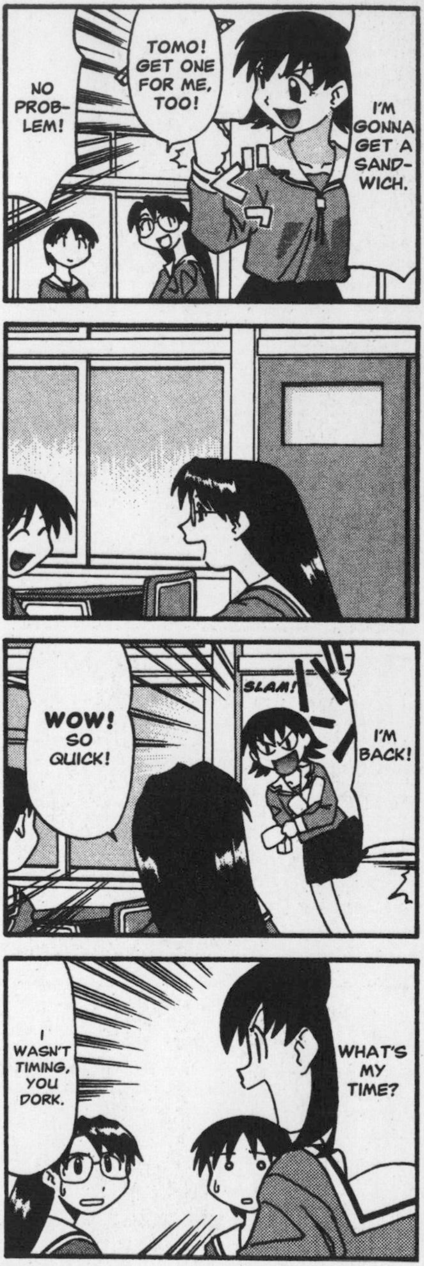
I'M GONNA GET A SANDWICH.
TOMO! GET ONE FOR ME, TOO!
NO PROBLEM!
I'M BACK!
SLAM!
WOW! SO QUICK!
WHAT'S MY TIME?
I WASN'T TIMING, YOU DORK.

ALL RIGHT! TOMO!

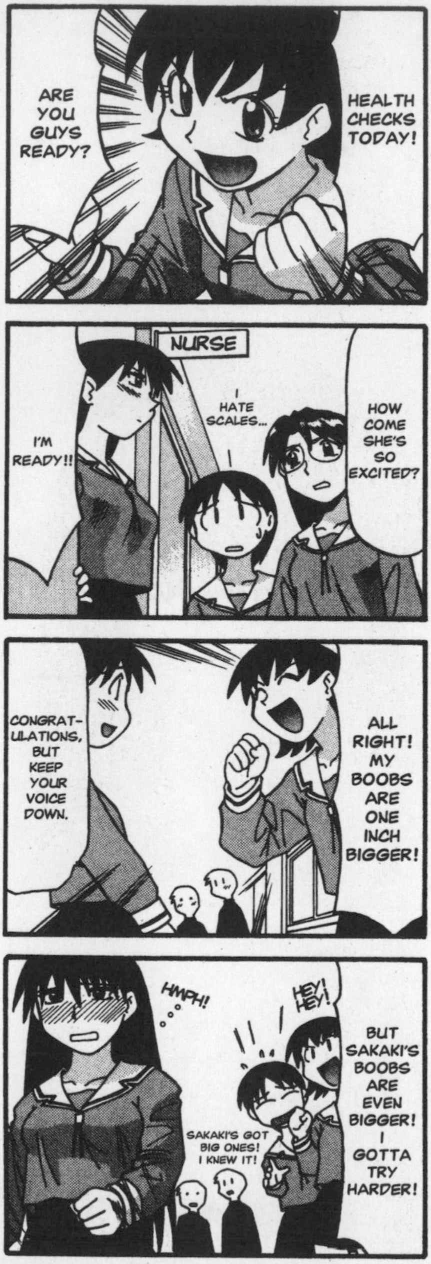
HEALTH CHECKS TODAY!
ARE YOU GUYS READY?
NURSE
HOW COME SHE'S SO EXCITED?
I HATE SCALES...
I'M READY!!
ALL RIGHT! MY BOOBS ARE ONE INCH BIGGER!
CONGRATULATIONS, BUT KEEP YOUR VOICE DOWN.
BUT SAKAKI'S BOOBS ARE EVEN BIGGER! I GOTTA TRY HARDER!
HEY! HEY!
SAKAKI'S GOT BIG ONES! I KNEW IT!
HMPH!

HEALTH FIRST!

4 APRIL PART-2

AZU MANGA DAIOH

I HATE CLEANING

PILES OF STUFF

YUKARI! DO SOMETHING ABOUT THIS MESS!

ALL RIGHT, THEN. GIVE ME MY DICTIONARY BACK.

NO PROBLEM!

NOT A PROBLEM. I KNOW WHAT'S WHERE.

GOT IT!

CRASH TUMBLE

WHY ARE YOU SO MAD?

HERE!

JEEZ! JUST TAKE IT!

WHICH SIDE ARE YOU ON?

STUDENTS LIKE HER.

MISS KUROSAWA (IN CHARGE OF PE)

THAT WOULD BE...

WHO DO YOU LIKE BEST, MISS YUKARI OR MISS KUROSAWA?

...UM, MISS YUKARI.

REALLY! YOU LIKE WEIRDOS, HUH?

TEENY-TINY CHIYO-CHAN

SHE ENTERED HIGH SCHOOL STUDENT AT AGE 10.

CHIYO-CHAN IS VERY SMART

CAN I HAVE THE LUNCH SPECIAL, PLEASE?

LUNCH SPECIAL

BUT...

YOU GOTTA EAT MORE TO GROW MORE!

WELL, I'M...

OH... YOU'RE SO SHORT!

HAP-PENS ALL THE TIME.

THAT LADY OVER THERE...

WHY SO MUCH?

A SECRET

WHAT KIND OF STUDENT WAS MISS YUKARI?

HAH HAH HAH!

MISS KUROSAWA AND MISS YUKARI WERE CLASS-MATES, RIGHT?

A LOVE LETTER, A LOVE LETTER! ♪

SO MANY STORIES...

LO-LO-LO-LO LOVE LETTER! ♪

は？ WHAT?

I GUESS MISS YUKARI HAS SOME-THING ON HER...

UM, JUST A NORMAL STUDENT, I GUESS...

......

SCARY!

WHO DIDN'T BRING THEIR HOMEWORK!

BOP BOP

SORRY... I FORGOT...

AWWW...

HE LIKES 'EM YOUNG.

HE LIKES 'EM YOUNG.

FLINCH

TAP

TONGUE TWISTER

YES... I'M NOT GOOD AT...

YOU'RE GOOD AT EVERYTHING! DO YOU HAVE ANY WEAKNESSES?

I'M NOT GOOD AT TONGUE TWISTERS!

RUGGY RUMPER BABY. RUMPER

RUBBER BABY RUGGY BUMPER

RUBBER BABY BUGGY BUMPER

AH... YOU'RE SO DAMN CUTE!

HE HE HE

OUCH!

WHAT HAPPENED TO YOUR HAND?

IT WAS... IN A BAD MOOD...

· · · · ·

SHE GOT IN A FIGHT...?

PETTING

CHOMP!

NEVER GIVE UP ON YOUR DREAM!

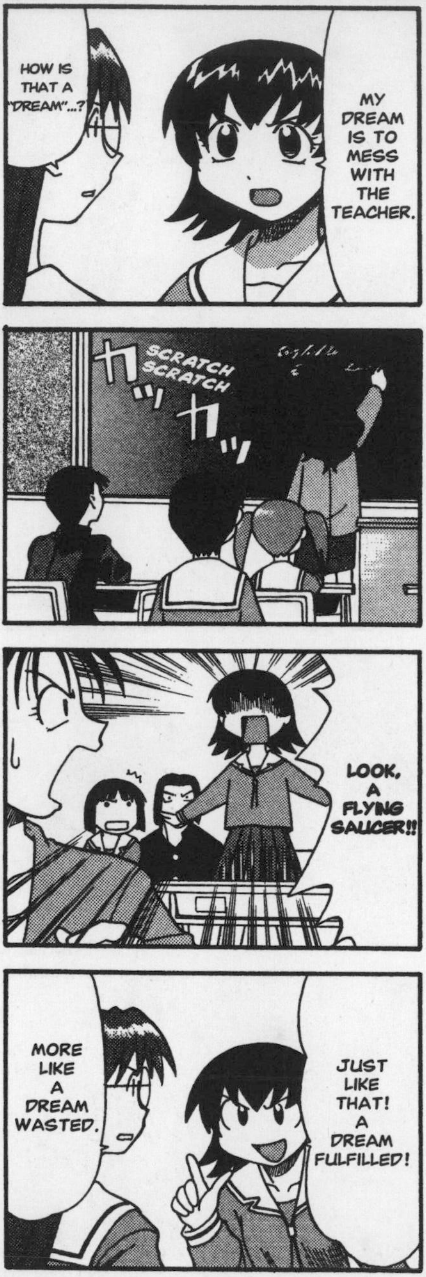
MY DREAM IS TO MESS WITH THE TEACHER.
HOW IS THAT A "DREAM"...?
SCRATCH SCRATCH
LOOK, A FLYING SAUCER!!
JUST LIKE THAT! A DREAM FULFILLED!
MORE LIKE A DREAM WASTED.

WHY?

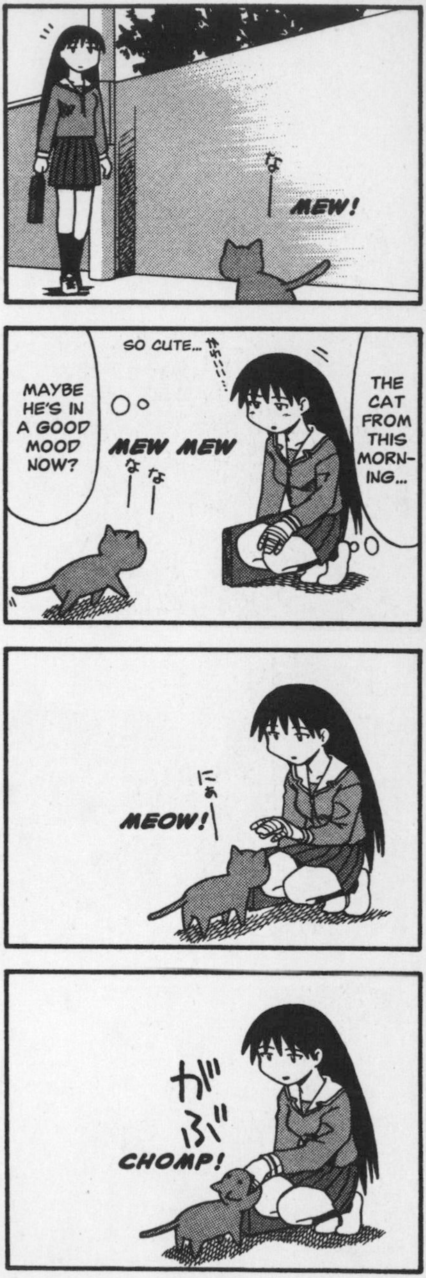
な
MEW!
SO CUTE...
THE CAT FROM THIS MORNING...
MAYBE HE'S IN A GOOD MOOD NOW?
MEW MEW
MEOW!
がぶ
CHOMP!

BUNNY CLUB

TOO MUCH ENERGY

TIE GAME

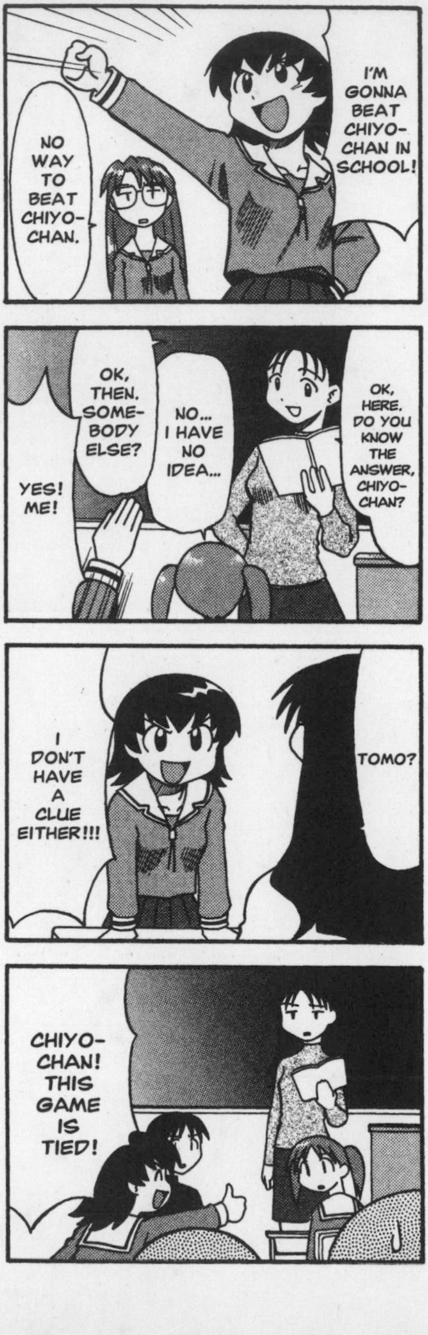
I'M GONNA BEAT CHIYO-CHAN IN SCHOOL!
NO WAY TO BEAT CHIYO-CHAN.
OK, HERE. DO YOU KNOW THE ANSWER, CHIYO-CHAN?
NO... I HAVE NO IDEA...
OK, THEN. SOMEBODY ELSE?
YES! ME!
TOMO?
I DON'T HAVE A CLUE EITHER!!!
CHIYO-CHAN! THIS GAME IS TIED!

THE 100-METER DASH!

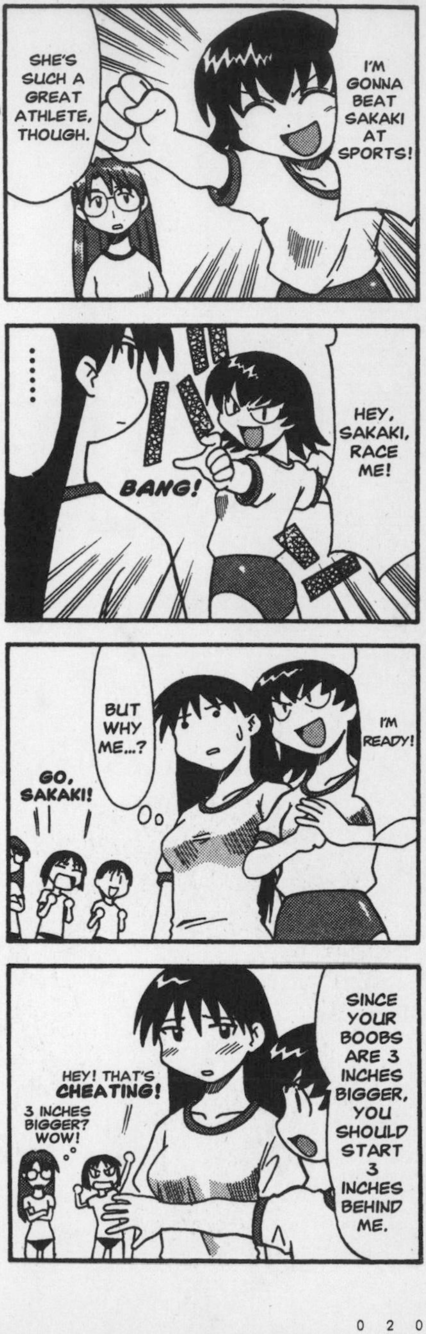
I'M GONNA BEAT SAKAKI AT SPORTS!
SHE'S SUCH A GREAT ATHLETE, THOUGH.
HEY, SAKAKI, RACE ME!
BANG!
......
I'M READY!
BUT WHY ME...?
GO, SAKAKI!
SINCE YOUR BOOBS ARE 3 INCHES BIGGER, YOU SHOULD START 3 INCHES BEHIND ME.
HEY! THAT'S CHEATING!
3 INCHES BIGGER? WOW!

TOMO-CHAN

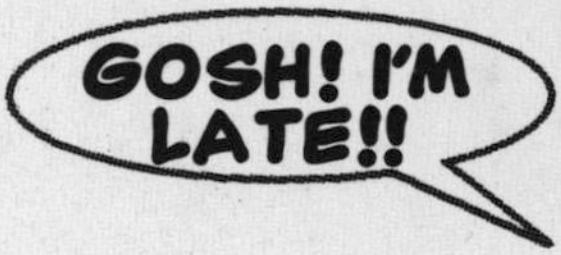
GOSH! I'M LATE!!

YUKARI COMMUTES BY BIKE

WHAT?

MAN! I'LL BE LATE!

MY CHAIN CAME OFF!

I'LL BE LATE!

GLARE

WHAT ARE YOU DOING MISS YUKARI?

PLUS, IT GIVES ME AN EXCUSE TO BE LATE!

RELAX! I'LL FIX IT FOR YOU.

WAIT! MY BIKE!

ZOOM!

AZU MANGA DAIOH

5 MAY PART-1

NERVOUS

YOU LITTLE BRAT!

WANT A CAR?

HUH?

REALLY?

I HEARD THIS MOVIE'S CUTE.

捨て猫物語

SURE!

ONE CHILD

1000

OK!

ONE HIGH-SCHOOL STUDENT.

HUH?

CHIYO-CHAN'S SUNDAY

HI, GUYS!

CHIYO-CHAN! WE'RE HERE!

(I NEED TO GET MONEY FROM MOM.)

WITHOUT OUR PARENTS?

SURE

LET'S GO SEE A MOVIE TODAY!

TEE-HEE

JUST LIKE A HIGH-SCHOOL GIRL! GETS TO GO TO MOVIES ALONE...

WOW! COOL!

(SPENDING HER OWN POCKET MONEY!)

I EVEN WENT TO MCDONALD'S AFTER SCHOOL ONE DAY.

WOW!

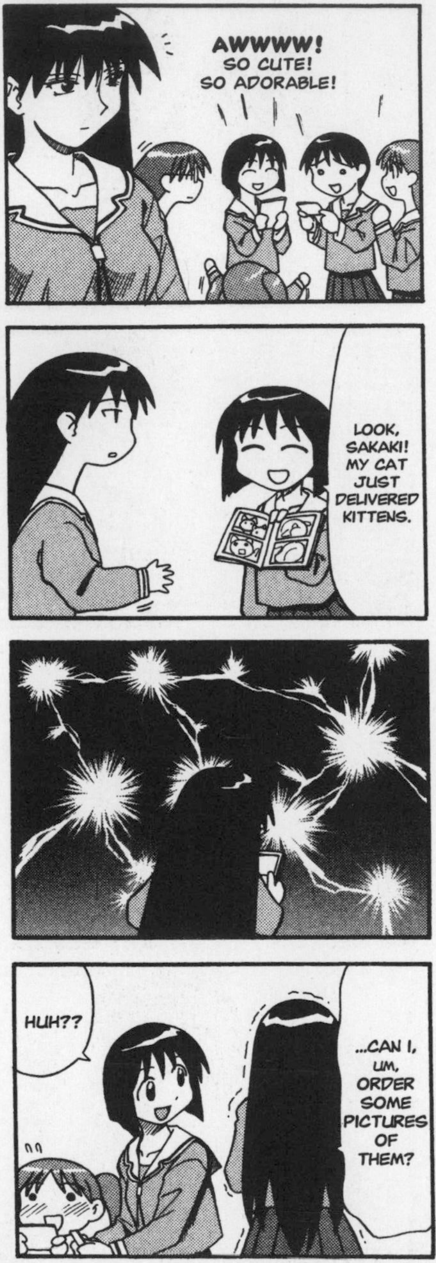
AWWWW!
SO CUTE!
SO ADORABLE!
LOOK, SAKAKI! MY CAT JUST DELIVERED KITTENS.
HUH??
...CAN I, UM, ORDER SOME PICTURES OF THEM?

GREAT MOVIE!

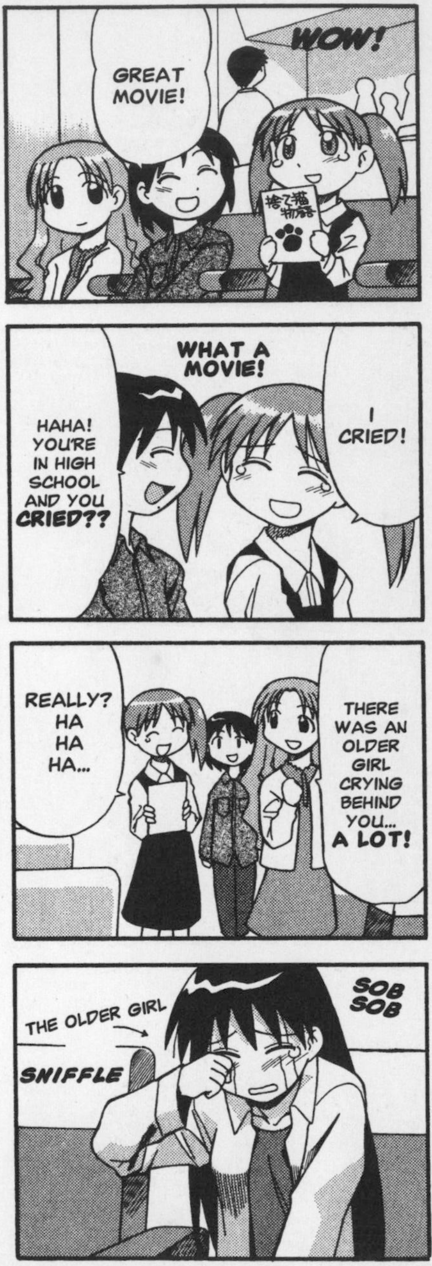
GREAT MOVIE!
WOW!
捨て猫物語
WHAT A MOVIE!
I CRIED!
HAHA! YOU'RE IN HIGH SCHOOL AND YOU CRIED??
REALLY? HA HA HA...
THERE WAS AN OLDER GIRL CRYING BEHIND YOU... A LOT!
SOB SOB
THE OLDER GIRL
SNIFFLE

RECOMMENDED PETS

DOESN'T KNOW ABOUT COMPUTERS →

WHAT'S AN E-PET?

WHAT DOES THE "E" MEAN? ELECTRIC? REMOTE-CONTROLLED PET?

CAN'T STOP THINKING ABOUT IT... →

WHAT'S THAT?

KIND OF...

DO YOU LIKE CATS?

NO. MY PARENTS WON'T ALLOW IT.

DO YOU HAVE A CAT AT HOME?

WHY DON'T YOU GET AN E-PET?

BUT WHAT'S AN E-PET...?

SURE!

KAORIN! COME HERE!

ANOTHER ANNOYING GIRL?!

NOT WHAT I THOUGHT IT WAS

THE GIRL FROM OSAKA

WOW, THE OSAKAN!

HERE'S THE NEW STUDENT, AYUMU KASUGA

NICE TO MEET YOU.

NO, NOT LIKE THAT.

I'M AYUMU KASUGA.

(NOBODY SPEAKS LIKE THAT IN OSAKA...)

YOU CAN SAY "YO, HOW YOU DOIN'?" IF YOU WANT.

RELAX! SPEAK LIKE YOURSELF!

"YO, HOW YOU DOIN'?"

GO AHEAD! SAY IT

FUHGEDDABOUDIT!

(WHY SHOULD WE...?)

LET'S TRY AND TALK LIKE HER!

SHE'S FROM OSAKA, SO I'LL BET SHE TALKS FUNNY!

DO I HAVE TO?

SAY "FUHGEDDABOUDIT", CAPISCE?

THAT'S SOOOO FUNNY!!

UAAAH! HAH HAHAHA!

FUHGEDDABOUDIT!

FUHGEDDABOUDIT!

MAYBE WE'RE MAKING TOO MUCH OF THIS...

THERE SHOULD BE A MEATBALL SANDWICH IN THERE!

SHOW ME YOUR LUNCH BOX.

AM I A PHONY OSAKAN?

THAT'S A STEREOTYPE!

YEAH, WE CALL IT MICKEY D'S.

IN OSAKA, YOU CALL MCDONALD'S "MICKEY D'S"?

OH...

NO, NOT EVERYONE'S LIKE THAT.

YOU'RE QUIET. I THOUGHT OSAKA PEOPLE WERE LOUD AND ANNOYING.

YEAH, THAT'S THE SPIRIT!

AH, FUHGEDDABOUDIT!

HUH?!

YOU'RE A PHONY!

I DON'T CARE.

AZU MANGA DAIOH

5 MAY PART-2

GOOD NEWS! MY BEST FRIEND'S GETTING MARRIED.

THAT'S WHY WE'RE HAVING A QUIZ TODAY!

WHAT!? WHY!?

SHUT UP!

SILENCE

TAP TAP

ANOTHER ONE GETTING MARRIED, HUH

EXCUSE?

MISS YUKARI'S LATE!
YAAH!
NO CLASS?!
BLAH BLAH!!
SHE'S ALWAYS LATE!
SLAM!
CLASS IS NOT CAN-CELLED!
SHE'S HERE!
I WENT TO BUY A PLAY-STATION GAME DURING LUNCH.
HUFF PUFF
BUT THE LINE WAS REALLY LONG FOR A WEEKDAY!
ALL THE COLLEGE KIDS SKIPPING LECTURES! THAT'S WHY I WAS LATE!
THAT'S WHY!
THAT'S YOUR EXCUSE?

A LESSON

I WENT TO THE WEDDING.
OH, SHIT!
ANOTHER QUIZ?!
HEH
HEH HEH HE-HE-HE...
FOOLS RUSH IN...

ON THE BALL!

IN OSAKA, PEOPLE TOLD ME I WAS SLOW AND AIRHEADED.

KASUGA

KASUGA!!

ON THE BALL!

I'VE GOTTA GET ON THE BALL NOW THAT I'M AT A NEW SCHOOL.

NO...

OH...

WEREN'T YOU LISTENING?

ON THE BALL...

WAKE UP! OK, NEXT! OKAWA!

DREAM WORLD

THAT I DO!

MISS YUKARI, YOU HAVE A PLAY STATION?

YOU CAN FORGET ABOUT THE REAL WORLD.

PLAY STATION GAMES ARE FUN

DID SOMETHING HAPPEN TO HER...?

YOU CAN RESET ANY TIME YOU WANT.

GENIUS...

BUT... I WAS THE SLOWEST RUNNER IN OSAKA.

NO WAY I CAN LOSE! NOW THERE'S A GRADE-SCHOOL STUDENT IN CLASS!

OH NO, I LOST!

YOU'RE THE FIRST ONE TO LOSE TO CHIYO-CHAN. SHE'S JUST TOO SMART!

HUFF WHEEZE

は─は─

I GET IT...

CHIYO-CHAN? SHE'S A CHILD GENIUS. WHAT'S THE DEAL WITH HER?

SHE'S ONLY 10, BUT HERE SHE IS IN HIGH SCHOOL!

YEAH... NOT REALLY. I SEE. THERE WAS THIS GUY... A LITTLE KNOW-IT-ALL. SO IS SHE LIKE A SUPER KNOW-IT-ALL?

COMPUTER!

VOLLEYBALL PRACTICE

A BUNNY

IS THERE A CAT HERE?

NO!! NO!!!

A BIG BUNNY

WOW...

WHAT'S THAT?

I WON IT AT THE MALL.

HI, SAKAKI!

THANKS!

MY... PLEAS- URE.

HUG

I'LL HELP YOU CARRY IT.

CHOMP!

CHOMP!

MID-TERMS

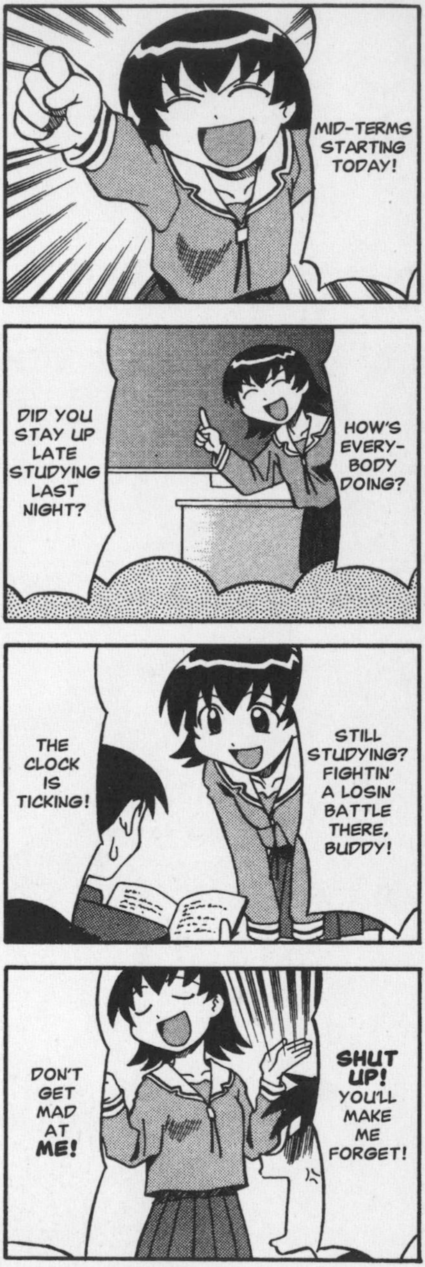
MID-TERMS STARTING TODAY!
HOW'S EVERY-BODY DOING?
DID YOU STAY UP LATE STUDYING LAST NIGHT?
STILL STUDYING? FIGHTIN' A LOSIN' BATTLE THERE, BUDDY!
THE CLOCK IS TICKING!
SHUT UP! YOU'LL MAKE ME FORGET!
DON'T GET MAD AT ME!

LET ME TELL YOU SOMETHING

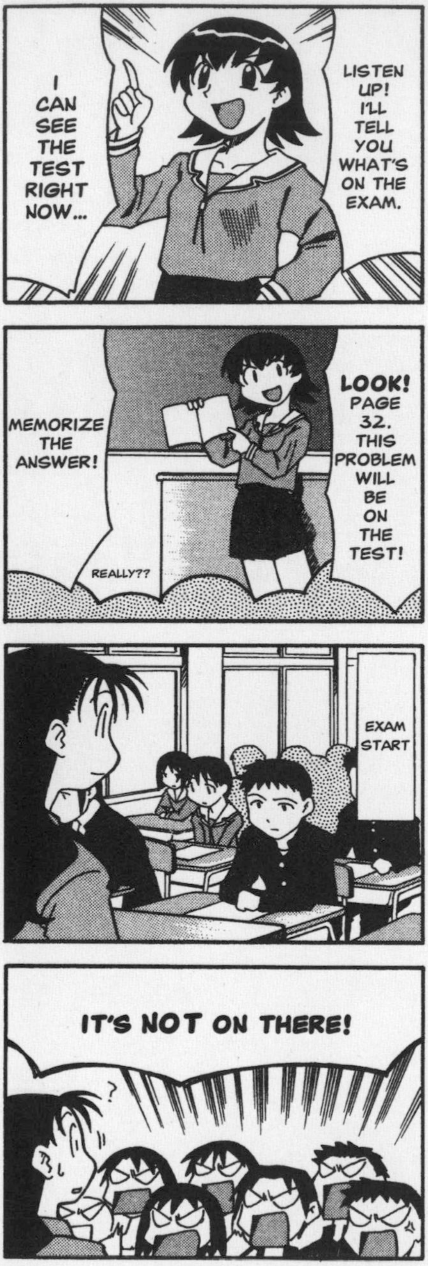
LISTEN UP! I'LL TELL YOU WHAT'S ON THE EXAM.
I CAN SEE THE TEST RIGHT NOW...
LOOK! PAGE 32. THIS PROBLEM WILL BE ON THE TEST!
MEMORIZE THE ANSWER!
REALLY??
EXAM START
IT'S NOT ON THERE!

SAKAKI

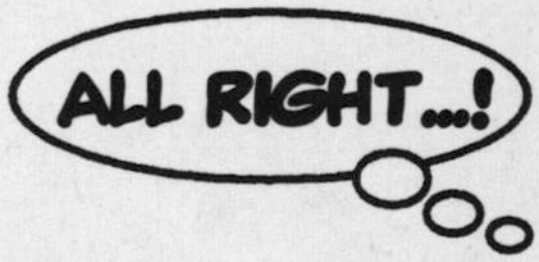
ALL RIGHT...!

WORKING GIRL

DING-DONG!

AZU MANGA DAIOH

6 JUNE

OK, OK! HOLD ON JUST A SEC! YUKARI! MINAMO'S HERE!

GOOD MORN-ING! MINAMO HERE!

?

WHY DON'T YOU WAKE ME UP, MOM? NOW I'M LATE!

BANG

BUT I WOKE YOU!

RATTLE CRASH

CLICK

YO.

YO.

BEST FRIENDS

OH, MR. GOTO! DON'T BE SILLY...

MISS TANIZAKI, YOU GET ALONG WELL WITH YOUR STUDENTS.

WHAT DO YOU DO IN CLASS?

MAYBE YOU COULD GIVE ME A FEW POINTERS?

HUH?

WELL, TODAY WE TALKED ABOUT THE BOYS WE HATED THE MOST. EVERYONE ENJOYED THAT.

THE COMMUTE

EVER SINCE SHE BOUGHT HER NEW CAR, MINAMO'S BEEN GIVING YUKARI RIDES TO SCHOOL.

PURR

YUKARI USUALLY SLEEPS THE WHOLE WAY.

ZZZZZZ...

HUH...? WHAT HAPPENED? ARE WE THERE YET?

DAMNIT!!

THE SWIMMING POOL

WHAT IS GENIUS?

RIBBON

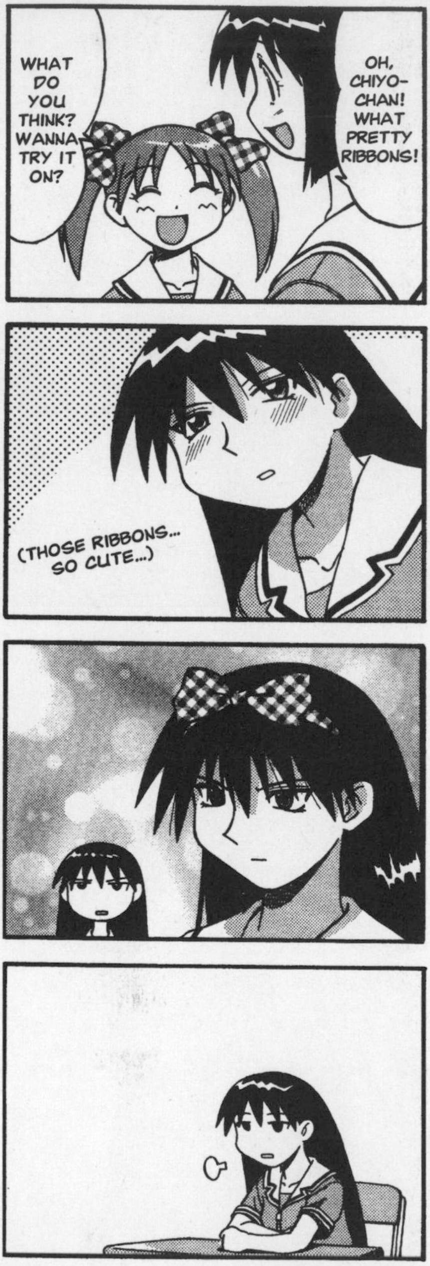

OH, CHIYO-CHAN! WHAT PRETTY RIBBONS!
WHAT DO YOU THINK? WANNA TRY IT ON?
(THOSE RIBBONS... SO CUTE...)

DELUSIONS

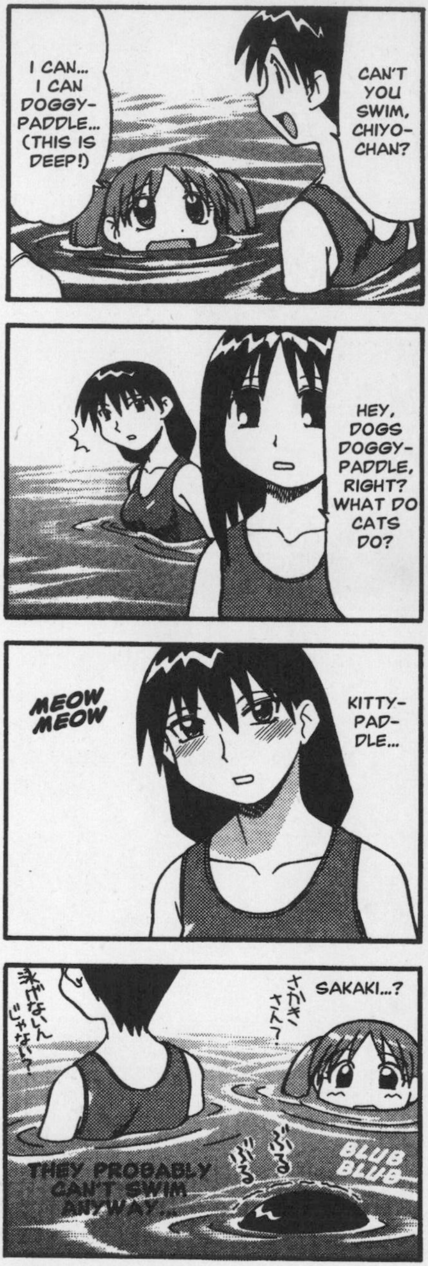

CAN'T YOU SWIM, CHIYO-CHAN?
I CAN... I CAN DOGGY-PADDLE... (THIS IS DEEP!)
HEY, DOGS DOGGY-PADDLE, RIGHT? WHAT DO CATS DO?
MEOW MEOW
KITTY-PAD-DLE...
SAKAKI...?
さかきさん?
泳げないんじゃない?
THEY PROBABLY CAN'T SWIM ANYWAY...
ぶるぶる
BLUB BLUB

I WANNA PET IT, TOO!

WHAT A DIRTY TRICK

I DID IT!

PLOP

SNAP!

HUH?

HEHE...

JUST 'CUZ SHE SPLIT HER CHOPSTICKS PERFECTLY? THAT'S IT?

HEHE...

HUH?

WHAT SHOULD I DO?

WHAT SHOULD I DO? I DON'T KNOW ANYBODY IN MY UHTHA CLASSES, NEITHA!

OH NO! I FUHGOT MY ENGLISH BOOK!

THAT'S IT! I'LL TELL THE TEACHA I ACCIDENTALLY BROUGHT ONE FROM OSAKA. MAYBE SHE'LL LET IT GO...

(NOT A VERY CONVINCING EXPLANATION...)

REALLY? WHAT BOOK DID THEY USE IN OSAKA? I'D LIKE TO SEE IT.

UM, TEACHA? I ACCIDEN- TALLY BROUGHT THE BOOK I HAD IN OSAKA, SO...

WHAT?!

UH, UH...UMM MM... I DON' GOT IT.

THE TRAP

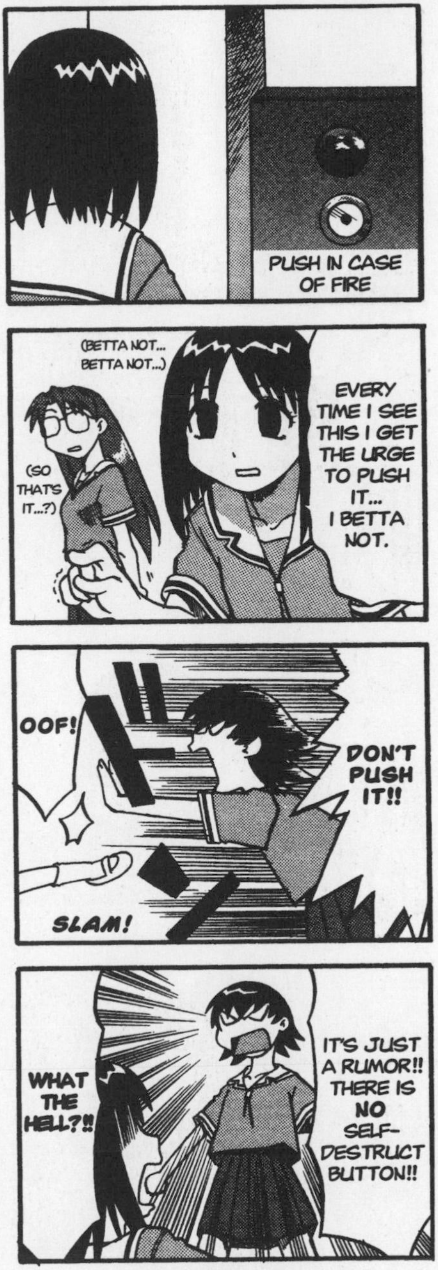
PUSH IN CASE OF FIRE
EVERY TIME I SEE THIS I GET THE URGE TO PUSH IT... I BETTA NOT.
(BETTA NOT... BETTA NOT...)
(SO THAT'S IT...?)
DON'T PUSH IT!!
OOF!
SLAM!
IT'S JUST A RUMOR!! THERE IS NO SELF-DESTRUCT BUTTON!!
WHAT THE HELL?!!

RUN AWAY!

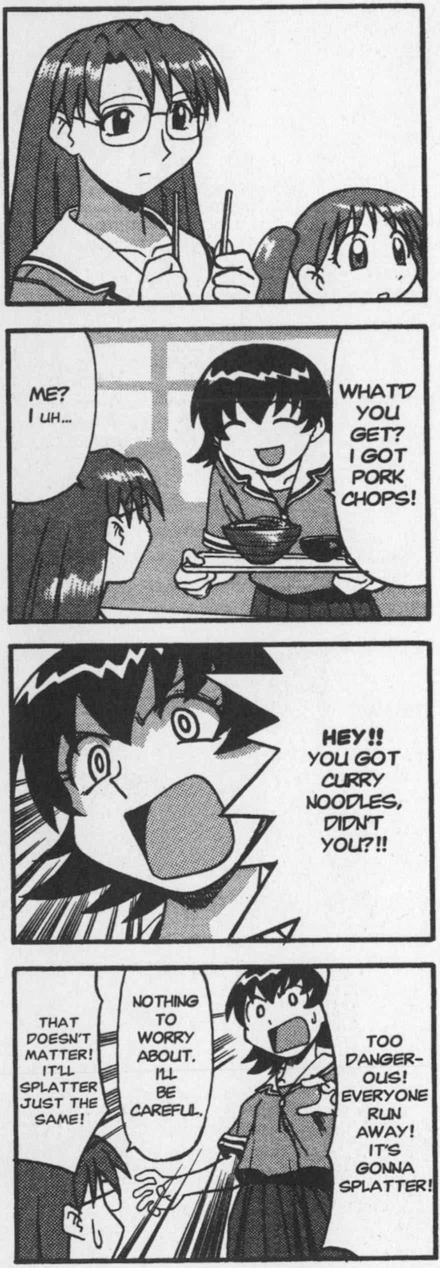
WHAT'D YOU GET? I GOT PORK CHOPS!
ME? I UH...
HEY!! YOU GOT CURRY NOODLES, DIDN'T YOU?!!
TOO DANGER-OUS! EVERYONE RUN AWAY! IT'S GONNA SPLATTER!
NOTHING TO WORRY ABOUT. I'LL BE CAREFUL.
THAT DOESN'T MATTER! IT'LL SPLATTER JUST THE SAME!

OSAKA

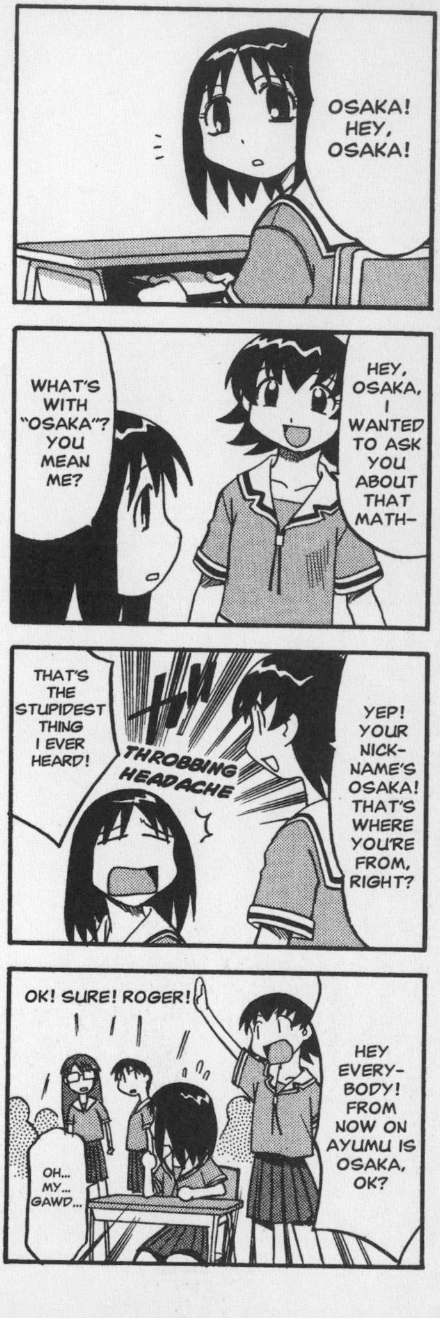
OSAKA! HEY, OSAKA!
HEY, OSAKA, I WANTED TO ASK YOU ABOUT THAT MATH-
WHAT'S WITH "OSAKA"? YOU MEAN ME?
YEP! YOUR NICK-NAME'S OSAKA! THAT'S WHERE YOU'RE FROM, RIGHT?
THROBBING HEADACHE
THAT'S THE STUPIDEST THING I EVER HEARD!
HEY EVERY-BODY! FROM NOW ON AYUMU IS OSAKA, OK?
OK! SURE! ROGER!
OH... MY... GAWD...

NAMING

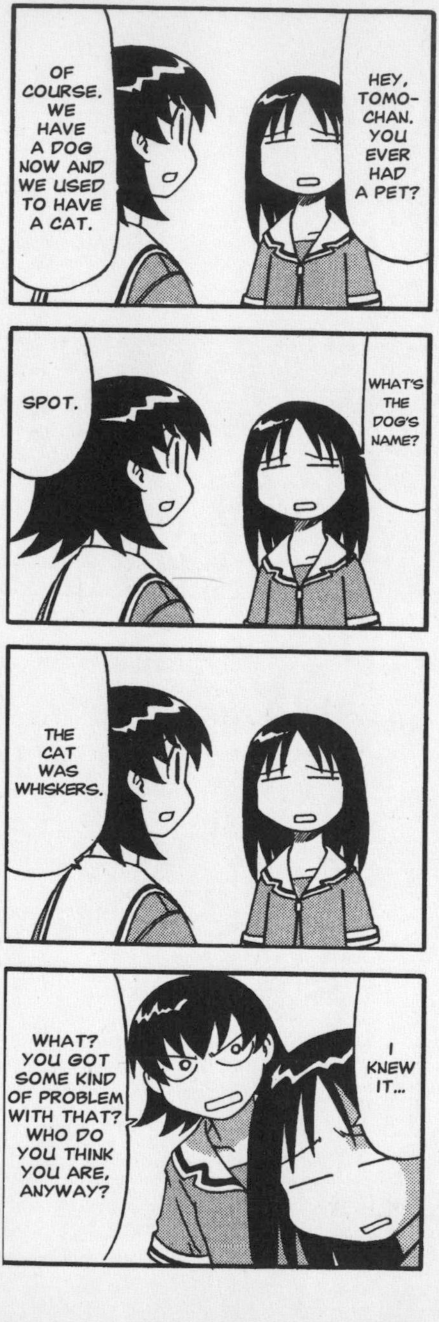
HEY, TOMO-CHAN. YOU EVER HAD A PET?
OF COURSE. WE HAVE A DOG NOW AND WE USED TO HAVE A CAT.
WHAT'S THE DOG'S NAME?
SPOT.
THE CAT WAS WHISKERS.
I KNEW IT...
WHAT? YOU GOT SOME KIND OF PROBLEM WITH THAT? WHO DO YOU THINK YOU ARE, ANYWAY?

CHIYO-CHAN

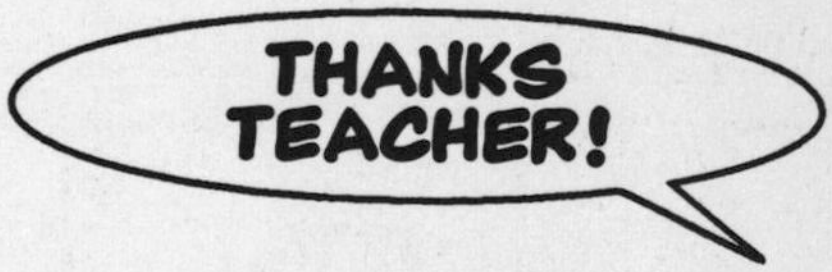
THANKS TEACHER!

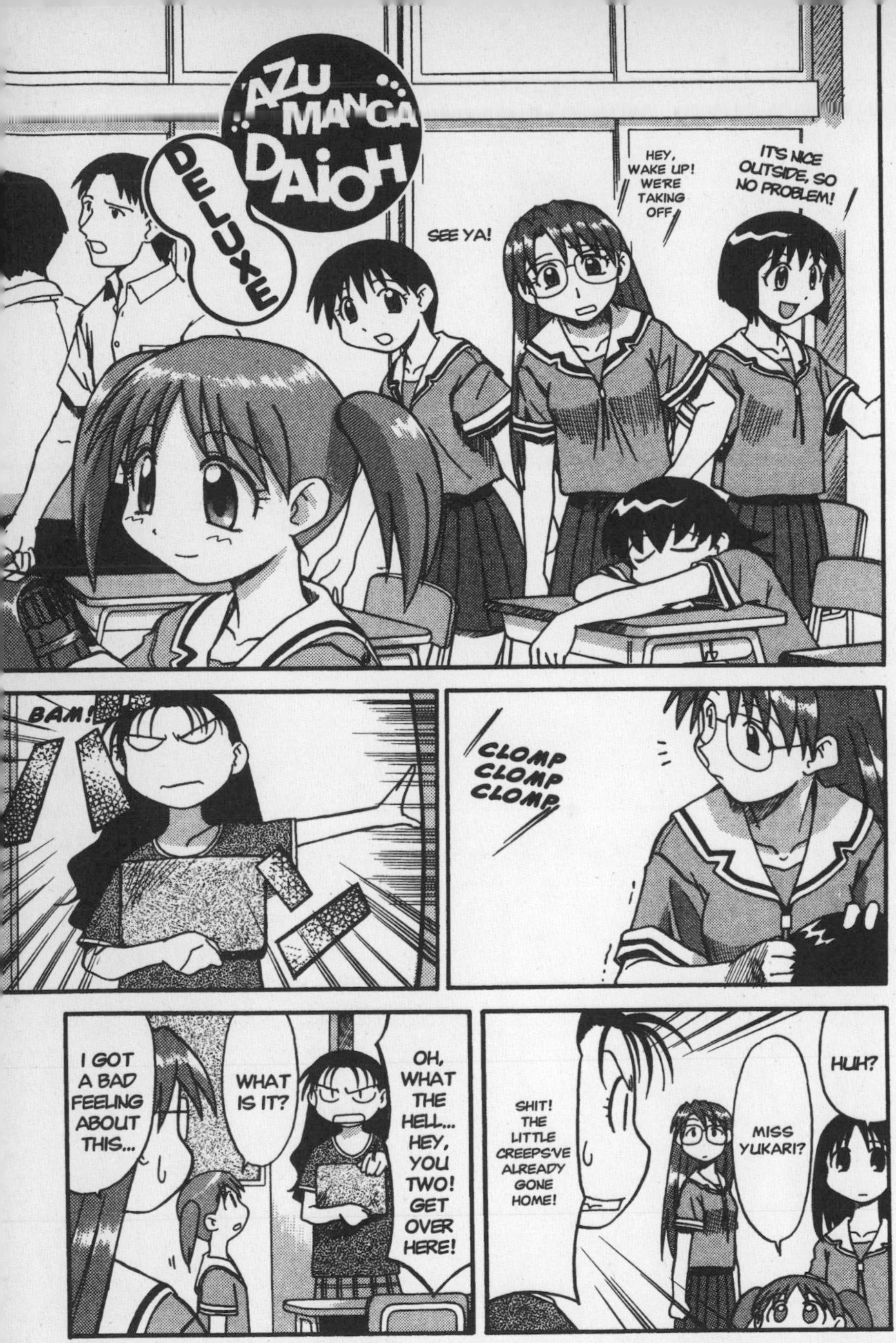
AZU MANGA DAIOH DELUXE
SEE YA!
HEY, WAKE UP! WE'RE TAKING OFF
IT'S NICE OUTSIDE, SO NO PROBLEM!
BAM!
CLOMP CLOMP CLOMP
I GOT A BAD FEELING ABOUT THIS...
WHAT IS IT?
OH, WHAT THE HELL... HEY, YOU TWO! GET OVER HERE!
SHIT! THE LITTLE CREEPS'VE ALREADY GONE HOME!
MISS YUKARI?
HUH?

SCUFF
SCUFF

SOMETHING NASTY?

WHAT IS IT?!

ACTUALLY, I JUST FOUND THIS.

AHHHH!!

WHIRL

A KITTY?!

WHADDAYA MEAN "HUH"? HOW DO YOU THINK THIS LITTLE GUY'LL GET BY ON HIS OWN? HE'LL DIE UNLESS ONE OF YOU TAKES HIM HOME!

HE'S SLEEP-ING...

...HUH?

ONE OF YOU, TAKE THIS HOME!

SO THAT'S WHY IT'S MY RESPONSIBILITY AS AN EDUCATOR TO...UH...TO... WELL, YOU KNOW, ANYWAY...

I MEAN... UH, KITTIES ARE...UH, THEY'RE A GREAT LEARNING EXPERIENCE FOR YOUNG STUDENTS!

DON'T BE RIDICU-LOUS!

WHY DON'T YOU TAKE HIM HOME, MISS YUKARI?

NO WAY.

US, TOO. HOW 'BOUT SAKAKI?

WE ALREADY GOT A DOG.

MINE, NEITHER.

YEAH, MY PARENTS WILL NEVER GO FOR IT.

BUT WHAT SHOULD WE TELL OUR PARENTS...?

WOULD SOMEONE **PLEASE** TAKE THIS THING HOME?!!

(WHAT SHOULD I DO...?)

LITTLE MARCO IN *CUORE*... HE WAS LOOKING FOR HIS MOMMIE, TOO, JUST LIKE THIS LITTLE GUY!

...REMINDS ME OF SOMETHING

IT'S SO SAD... THE POOR LITTLE THING...

THAT'S IT! I'LL CALL HIM MARCO, LIKE IN THE STORY!

NAME: MARCO

ALREADY NAMING HIM, AND NOT EVEN KEEPING HIM...

WHAT WAS IT...? HMM...

HEY, FLUFFY! WAKE UP!

DON'T GIVE UP, MARCO!

ABSO-LUTELY NOT! IT'S NOT LIKE HE'S A GOLD-FISH!

YEAH! WE CAN SWITCH DAYS FOR FEEDING HIM, AND I DON'T MIND DOING THE POTTY-TRAINING!

THE WHOLE CLASS?

I KNOW! LET'S HAVE THE WHOLE CLASS KEEP HIM!

YOU'RE ALL SO SELFISH! I CAN'T BELIEVE YOU'RE JUST SITTING THERE! MAKES ME SO MAD...!!

COME ON, PEOPLE! ISN'T THERE **ANYONE** WHO'LL TAKE HIM HOME?

OHHH...

HEY, DON'T CHANGE THE SUBJECT!

I GUESS 'CUZ THEY LOOK LIKE A CAT'S TAILS.

YOU KNOW THEM CATTAILS THAT GROW NEXT TO THE RIVER? WHY DO THEY CALL 'EM THAT, I WONDA?

WHAT'S UP WITH "YUKARI BABY"??

HUH?!

ALL RIGHT, YUKARI **BABY**! I'LL TAKE CARE OF IT!

OF COURSE NOT! JUST JOKING!

YOU WOULDN'T...!!

WELL, IT'S NOT FUNNY!

YOU CAN'T!

WE LIVE CLOSE TO THE POUND, SO IT'S NO PROBLEM.

UH?

MEOW

LOOK HOW CUTE HE IS!

HEY, HE WOKE!

I'M GONNA PICK HIM UP!

WHOA~

ME, TOO!

I WANNA HOLD HIM, TOO! (STOP CRYING)

HES SOOO CUTE!!

UH, UH

FUSS FUSS

ME NEXT!

?

THUMP
THUMP
THUMP
THUMP

LIN, I DON'T KNOW...

SAKAKI, YOU WANNA HOLD HIM TOO?

THUMP
THUMP
THUMP
THUMP

WHOOSH

BOUNCE
BOUNCE

AAAAH!

WHAT THE—?!

ZIP
ZING

OOPS!

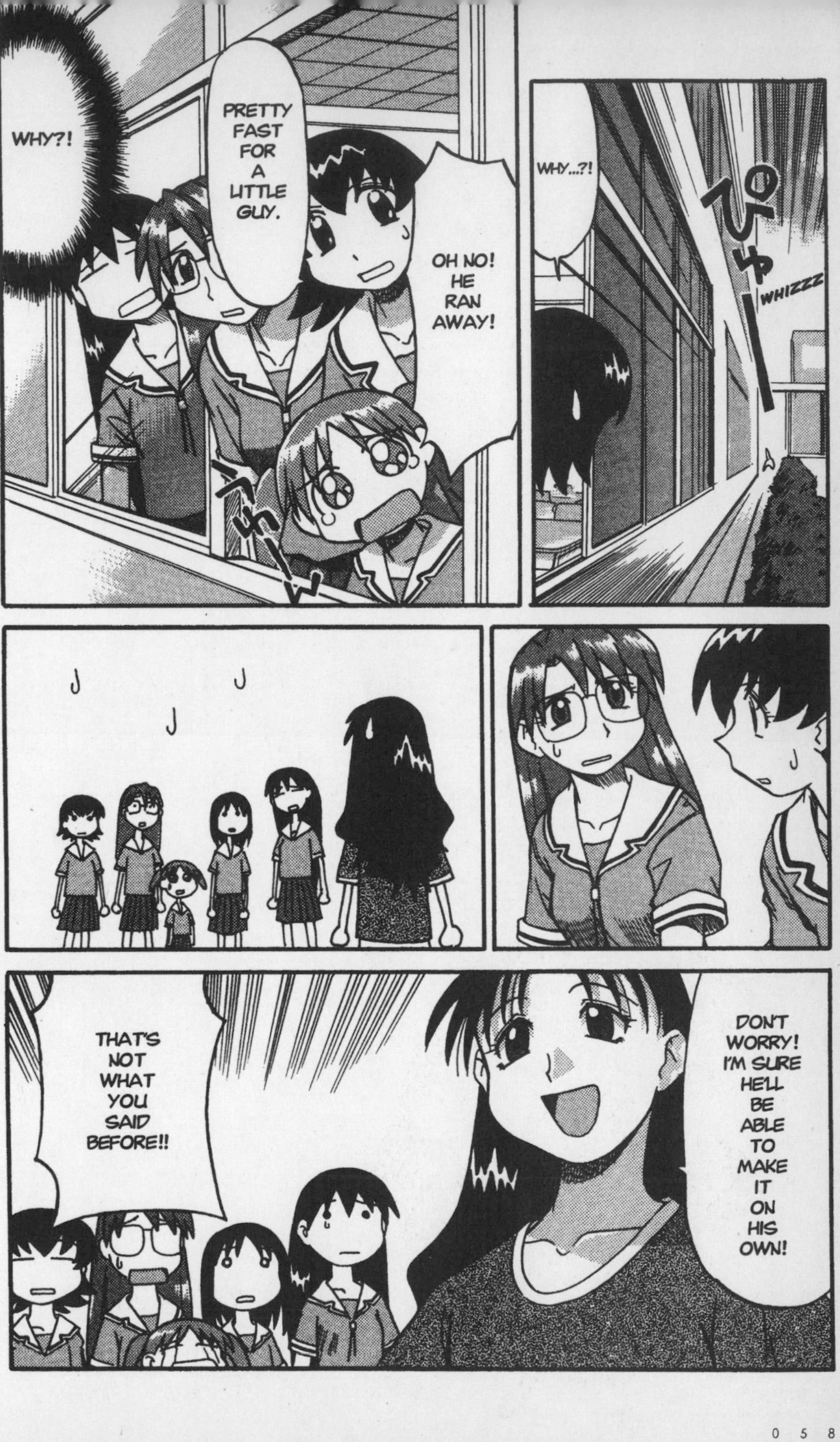
WHY...?!
WHIZZZ
OH NO! HE RAN AWAY!
PRETTY FAST FOR A LITTLE GUY.
WHY?!
DON'T WORRY! I'M SURE HE'LL BE ABLE TO MAKE IT ON HIS OWN!
THAT'S NOT WHAT YOU SAID BEFORE!!

MISS YUKARI

I'M NOT WRONG!!

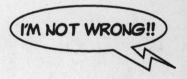

I HATE HIM

OH, WE WERE JUST TALKING ABOUT THIS GUY IN MY CLASS THAT WE HATE.

MISS TANIZAKI, YOU'RE HAVING A GOOD TIME! WHAT'S ALL THE RUCKUS?

HONESTLY, YOU'RE A **TEACHER**! I DON'T THINK YOU SHOULD BE DISCUSSING THAT HERE!

YOU KNOW, THE OTHER DAY HE...

ME, TOO!

I REALLY **HATE** THAT GUY!

MISS KUROSAWA GOT MAD

YOU CAN HAVE FUN ALL YOU WANT, BUT WHAT ARE YOU GONNA DO WHEN SOMEONE GETS HURT?

I'M SORRY...

HEY, NYAMO!

JUST BE CARE-FUL...

CAN'T YOU SEE I'M TALKING TO A STUDENT HERE?

HEY, NYAMO...I WANTED TO TELL YOU SOME-THING.

I TOLD YOU NOT TO CALL ME THAT AT SCHOOL!

MINAMO KUROSAWA ...WE CALL HER "NYAMO"

"NYAMO" ...?

MISS YUKARI GOT YELLED AT

YOU HAVEN'T CHANGED A BIT SINCE YOU WERE A STUDENT YOURSELF!

YOU'D BETTER START ACTING MORE LIKE A TEACHER, MISSIE!

OH, WELL IN THAT CASE, NO PROB-LEM!

IT'S ONE THING TO **ACT** FRIENDLY WITH YOUR STU-DENTS, BUT...

I'M JUST **PRETENDING** TO BE THEIR FRIEND, ANYWAY.

I JUST CAN'T

I'M SO BORED.

WHIRR

POP! RUSTLE RUSTLE

CREAK

STOP IT ALREADY!

YUKARI'S DRIVING

HEY, WILL YOU LET ME DRIVE YOUR CAR WHEN WE GO HOME?

ARE YOU SURE YOU WANT TO?

SURE. I PRACTICED ON MY DAD'S CAR THE OTHER DAY.

OKAY, NO PROB.

READY?

I WON'T CRASH THIS TIME.

WHAT'D YOU JUST SAY?

RIVAL?

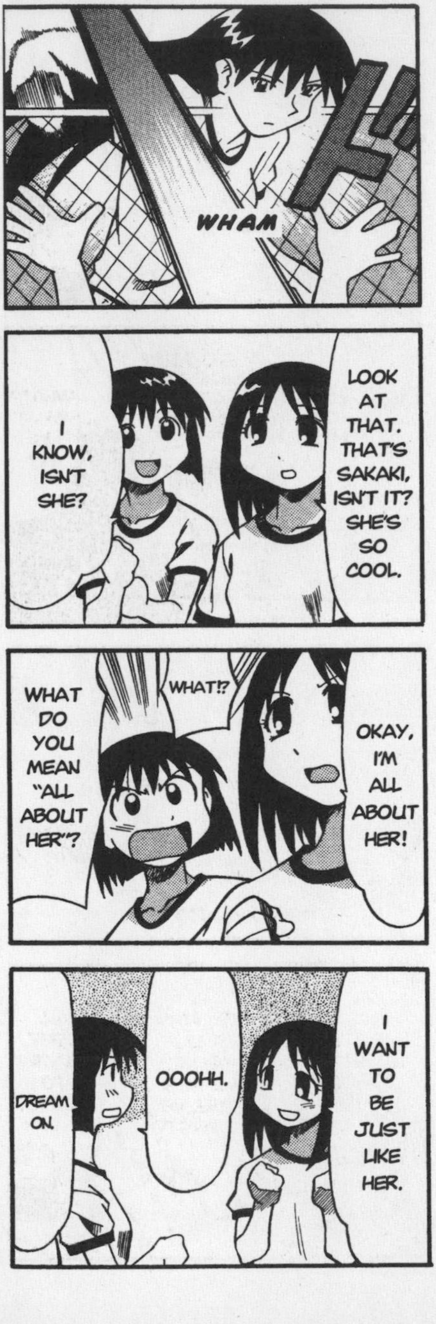

WHAM
LOOK AT THAT. THAT'S SAKAKI, ISN'T IT? SHE'S SO COOL.
I KNOW, ISN'T SHE?
OKAY, I'M ALL ABOUT HER!
WHAT!?
WHAT DO YOU MEAN "ALL ABOUT HER"?
I WANT TO BE JUST LIKE HER.
OOOHH.
DREAM ON.

VOLLEYBALL

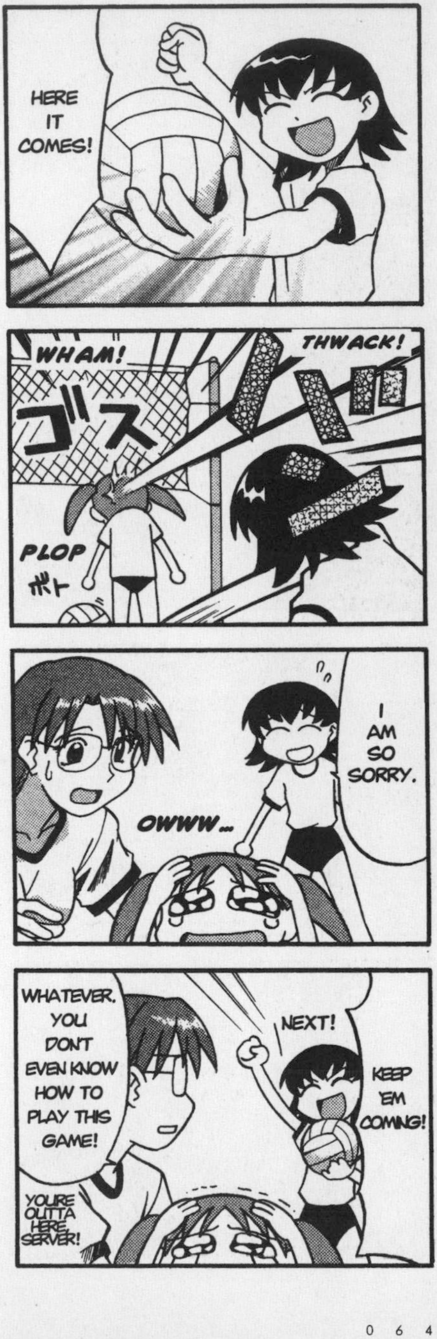

HERE IT COMES!
WHAM!
THWACK!
ゴス
バ
PLOP
ポト
OWWW...
I AM SO SORRY.
NEXT!
KEEP 'EM COMING!
WHATEVER. YOU DON'T EVEN KNOW HOW TO PLAY THIS GAME!
YOU'RE OUTTA HERE SERVER!

DEADLY WEAPON

EXCUSE ME.

TO CONTINUE ON IN OUR BOOKS...

WHAT IS IT?

OH MY GAWD!

I KILLED THAT ROACH WITH MY BOOK.

E-E-E-E-K!!

WHAT SHOULD I DO?

DON'T COME NEAR ME! I WILL KILL YOU!

NOOOO!

SCARED STIFF

YA~!

AND SO THAT'S WHY—

A ROACH!

SCOOT! SCRAPE! (CHAIRS MOVING BACK)

WHAT? WHAT IS IT?

WAAAA!

I'LL HANDLE THIS.

EEK!

GO, TOMO-CHAN!

SOMEBODY, STOMP ON IT!

KERSPLATT

DUNNO...

HEY, WHO LET OUT THAT BIG-ASS SCREAM AT FIRST?

ALL RIGHT, BACK TO CLASS.

PLAYING TRAIN STATION

NOT EXACTLY OSAKA

PUNISHMENT

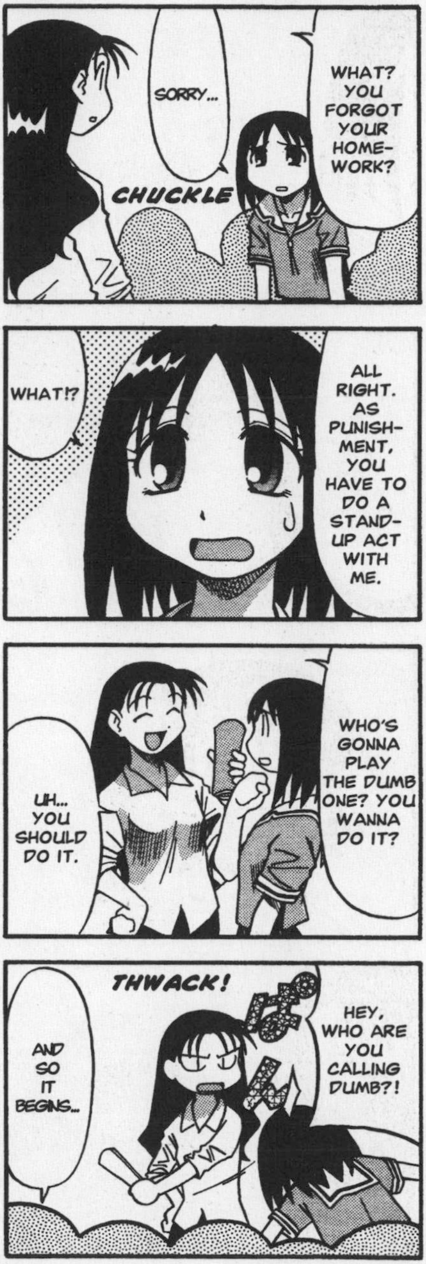
WHAT? YOU FORGOT YOUR HOMEWORK?
SORRY...
CHUCKLE
ALL RIGHT. AS PUNISHMENT, YOU HAVE TO DO A STAND-UP ACT WITH ME.
WHAT!?
WHO'S GONNA PLAY THE DUMB ONE? YOU WANNA DO IT?
UH... YOU SHOULD DO IT.
THWACK!
HEY, WHO ARE YOU CALLING DUMB?!
AND SO IT BEGINS...

PAIRS

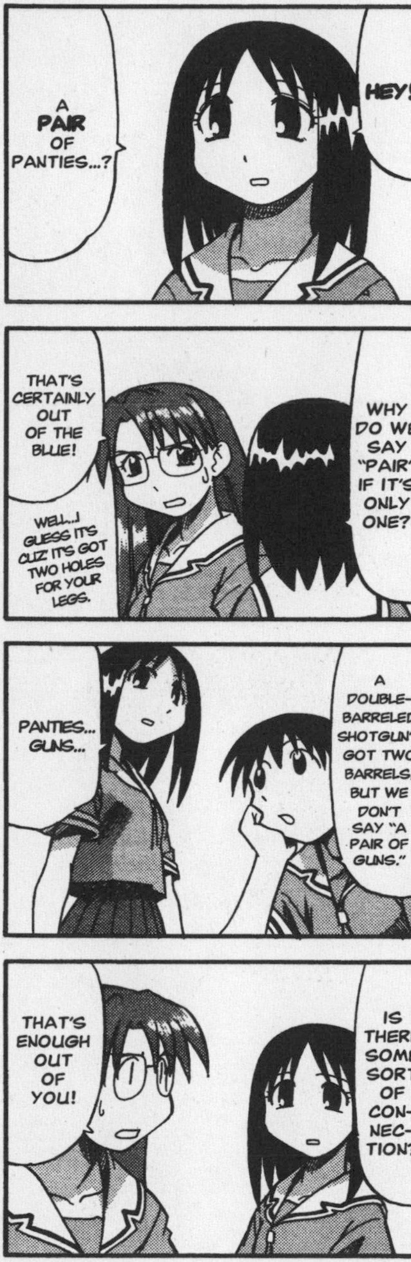
HEY!
A PAIR OF PANTIES...?
WHY DO WE SAY "PAIR" IF IT'S ONLY ONE?
THAT'S CERTAINLY OUT OF THE BLUE!
WELL...I GUESS ITS CUZ ITS GOT TWO HOLES FOR YOUR LEGS.
A DOUBLE-BARRELED SHOTGUN'S GOT TWO BARRELS, BUT WE DON'T SAY "A PAIR OF GUNS."
PANTIES... GUNS...
IS THERE SOME SORT OF CONNEC-TION?
THAT'S ENOUGH OUT OF YOU!

FROM KUROSAWA

MAKES NO SENSE

DON'T BE TOO SCARED, IT'S ONLY HEALTH AND P.E.

OKAY, LET'S START.

FINAL EXAM

GO ON A DIET?

I GOTTA LOSE SOME WEIGHT...

LET'S SAY WE EAT THE SAME AMOUNT OF FOOD, RIGHT?

YOU KNOW WHAT'S WEIRD?

I BELIEVE IN YOU! -KUROSAWA

IN YOUR CASE, IT'D JUST MAKE YOU TALL AND BUSTY.

YOU THINK...?

I'LL DO MY BEST...

COOL IT, ALREADY.

ISN'T THAT HILARIOUS? BWAA-HAAA-HAA!

IN MY CASE, IT'D GO RIGHT TO MY GUT!

BARELY...

OK EVERYONE, HERE ARE YOUR TESTS.

WHAT'S WITH THE FACE?

HEH HEH...

I THINK I DID OK ON THAT TEST. AIZAWA

WHY'D YOU STUDY SO HARD FOR P.E.?

YOU MIGHT NOT'VE NOTICED, BUT I STUDIED HARD FOR THAT P.E. TEST!

AHA HA HA HA...

YOU CHOSE WISELY.

SO I CAN COM-PETE WITH CHIYO-CHAN, OF COURSE!

SHUT IT!

HEY, I'VE BEEN MEANING TO TELL YOU THIS FOR A LONG TIME...

AHA HA HA... I DID HORRIBLE ON THAT TEST!

WHO? ME?

YEAH, YOU ARE...

YOU'RE LOUD AS HELL!

AND YOU KNOW WHAT THEY SAY...

I'M NOT LOUD, I'M MERRY!

NUTHIN' MERRY 'BOUT YOU...

"THE MORE THE MERRIER!"

TOMO / CHIYO WAR

HERE ARE TESTS FROM THE OTHER DAY.
AHA HA HA... THAT'S WHY I ONLY SCORED A 35!
WE HAD ENGLISH AND P.E. ON THE SAME DAY, DIDN'T WE?
YOU WANT A PIECE OF ME, YOU LITTLE TURD?

UNYIELDING

CHIYO-CHAN, WHAT'D YOU GET?
UH... A 92.
REALLY?
HA HA HA HA... I GOT A 100!
YOU WEREN'T LYING ABOUT STUDYING HARD.
SHE'S SO SILLY. I DON'T KNOW WHY SHE STUDIED SO HARD FOR THIS...
SHE LOOKS REALLY DISAPPOINTED...
......

OSAKA

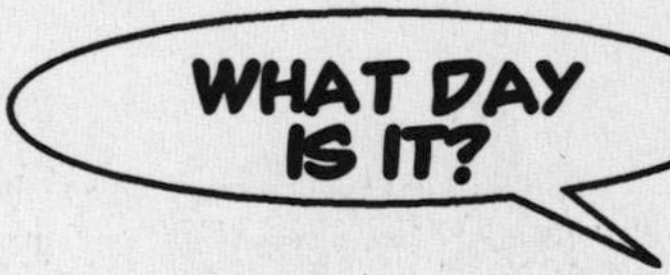
WHAT DAY
IS IT?

YUKARI'S SUMMER VACATION

HELLO!

AZU MANGA DAIOH

IT'S ALREADY EVENING!

UH... MORNING.

HUH?

YOU BEEN STAYING UP LATE?

IT SHOWS.

AT NIGHT? NO, I BEEN SLEEPING AT NIGHT, TOO.

LET'S GO TO THE POOL!

YUKARI'S PLAN

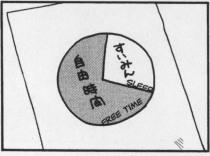

WEE!

PSHH! PSHHH! (INFLATING SHARK)

HEY, I SPENT GOOD MONEY ON THIS!

YOU GOT SOME NERVE WEARING THAT AT THE SCHOOL POOL.

SHARK!

BUT MAYBE IT'S TOO MUCH FOR THE YOUNG BOYS TO HANDLE...

PAY HER NO MIND.

SPLASH SPLASH

THAT WOMAN IN THE 8TH LANE IS OFF IN HER OWN WORLD...

I GUESS IT'S A MATTER OF TASTE...

OR I COULD WEAR A SCHOOL SWIM-SUIT... THEY MIGHT LIKE THAT BETTER.

STUDENT ID

TERIYAKI BURGER

YESSIR!

YOU'RE... A HIGH SCHOOL STUDENT?!

ALL RIGHT.

EXCUSE ME. I'D LIKE TO APPLY FOR A SUMMER JOB.

SHE MUST REALLY NEED THE MONEY.

SHE LOOKS LIKE AN GRADESCHOOLER...

I'LL DO MY BEST!

ALL RIGHT, WELCOME ABOARD!

I WANT A JOB, TOO!

AND WHO'S THIS LITTLE GIRL...?

IT'S NOT FOR ME

HEY, SAKAKI!

WELCOME TO MAGNE-TRON BURGER!

YES! MAY I TAKE YOUR ORDER?

YOU... WORK HERE?

KITTY CAT COMBO TOY INCLUDED!

セット

CHILDREN ONLY, PLEASE.

HUH?

SO, MY LITTLE COUSIN'S VISITING RIGHT NOW, AND...

KID CLERK

WHAT?!

WELCOME TO MAGNE-TRON BURGER!

WHAT?!

FOR HERE OR TO GO?

OK, THEN... ?

WE HAVE A SPECIAL ON THIS RIGHT NOW.

AM I ON CANDID CAMERA?

THANK YOU VERY MUCH!

JAGUAR

MAYBE.

SAKAKI IS MORE LIKE A JAGUAR THAN A HOUSE-CAT.

WHAT? A JAGUAR'S A JAGUAR.

IS A JAGUAR A TIGER?

NO, A JAGUAR!

A CHEE-TAH?

GOOD TIMING

WE HAVE THE PERFECT KID'S MEAL FOR YOUZ! THE KITTY CAT COMBO!

HEY, SAKAKI!

I'LL TAKE ONE.

AH, I'M JUST PLAYING WITCHA. AHA HA HA HA...

HAS THE SUMMER HEAT GONE TO YOUR HEAD?

NO, IT'S FOR MY COUSIN.

WHAT GIVES? I WAS JUST JOKIN'!

THANK YOU, COME AGAIN.

NOT WHAT WE EXPECTED...

TODAY, WE'LL BE VISITING CHIYO-CHAN'S HOME.

THE HOUSE IS ALL THE WAY IN THE BACK

NICE HOUSE!

JUST ACT NORMAL, OK.

MAYBE WE SHOULD'VE BROUGHT A GIFT OR SOMETHING...

YOU GOT IT ALL

SUMMER VACATION SPECIAL PROJECT— "SHOW US YOUR HOME!"

SHOOT, I FORGOT MY NOTEBOOK.

AND COPYING HER HOMEWORK WHILE I'M AT IT!

I CAN DO IT ON MY OWN.

AND A NICE BODY ON TOP OF THAT... WHAT DO YOU WANT FROM US?

PFFF, MUST BE NICE TO BE SO SMART!

INVITATION

WELCOME TO MY ROOM

THE USUAL SUSPECTS

AUGUST **8** PART-2

AZU MANGA DAIOH

WHATEVER...

GREAT WEATHER FOR GOING TO A SUMMER HOME!

BEAUTIFUL WEATHER!

YEAH, I RAN INTO HER AT THE LIBRARY THE OTHER DAY, SO I ASKED HER ALONG

CHIYO-CHAN, DID YOU INVITE SAKAKI, TOO?

YEAH!

YEAH!

GOOD JOB, CHIYO-CHAN!

I CALLED TO SEE IF I NEEDED PERMISSION AND THEY INSISTED ON COMING...

"THESE TWO!?"

BUT WHO THE HELL INVITED **THESE** TWO?

HEAVEN AND HELL

BUT, MISS YUKARI'S CAR HAS MORE ROOM, SO SHOULDN'T SHE TAKE THREE?

SO THEN, THREE WILL RIDE WITH ME AND THE OTHER TWO WITH YUKARI.

THE FEWER FATALITIES THE BETTER, RIGHT?

...

ROCK-PAPER-SCISSORS!

A FEW DENTS

YEAH, YOU'RE RIGHT....

HEY! WE'RE THE ONES DRIVING! FOR FREE, NO LESS!

OKAY, WHO WANTS TO RIDE WITH ME?!

MISS YUKARI...

WELL ACTUALLY, IT'S MY PARENTS' CAR, BUT...

FOR YOUR INFORMATION, MY CAR IS MORE EXPENSIVE THAN HERS.

BUT I **DO** WORRY!

BUT NOT TO WORRY

IT MIGHT HAVE A FEW DENTS...

HOW NOT TO SPLIT A WATERMELON

I SAW YOU

ABOUT DOLPHINS

SPEAKING OF THE OCEAN... I'VE ALWAYS WANTED TO RIDE A DOLPHIN.

RIGHT!

SOUNDS LOVELY...

BREAKING THE MOOD

WHAT THE—?!

HEY, YOU KNOW ABOUT HEMORRHOIDS...

...

WHICH ONE IS CORRECT?

YOU KNOW PEOPLE CALL IT HEMORHOIDS, BUT SOME PEOPLE CALL IT THE 'ROIDS.

WHO CARES?!

IF I LOOK IT UP IN THE DICTIONARY, WOULD IT BE UNDER HEMORRHOIDS OR THE 'ROIDS?

YUKARI GONE WILD

ABOUT DOLPHINS?

WELL, IT'S NIGHT TIME!

LET'S SHOOT OFF SOME FIREWORKS!

I BROUGHT SOME, TOO!

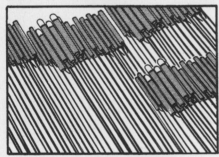

WHAT'S GOING ON, GUYS? YOU TWO ARE SPACING OUT.

FOR SOME REASON, SHE'S LOVED BOTTLE ROCKETS EVER SINCE SHE WAS A KID...

SHOOO! SHOOO! SHOOO! (BOTTLE ROCKETS SHOOTING IN AIR)

YIPPEE!

LOOKS FUN...

BUT WEREN'T WE JUST TALKING ABOUT...?

OH, I WAS JUST THINKING ABOUT HEMORRHOIDS.

YESSS!

DIRTY STORIES?

DO YOU KNOW ANY GOOD ONES?

OK, LET'S TELL SOME SCARY STORIES!

LET'S ASK THESE EXPERIENCED ADULTS!

HERE'S ONE.

NAH, NOTHING.

ALL THESE COCKROACHES CAME UP AND STARTED COVERING THE WHOLE—

THERE WAS THIS SUMMER HOME, AND ONE SUMMER...

GIVE US SOMETHING TO WORK WITH HERE!

IT'S NOT SO BAD LIVING ALONE.

THANKS FOR PLAYING! NOW TIME FOR DIRTY STORIES!

WHACK!

THE CONFESSION

YEAH, I GUESS SO.

IF THIS WAS A TV DRAMA, SOMEONE'D BE MURDERED JUST ABOUT NOW, HUH?

THE FIRST VICTIM'D BE TOMO-CHAN...

AND THEN, ONE BY ONE, EVERYONE'D BE KILLED.

HOW COME **YOU** GET TO BE THE KILLER?!

AND THE KILLER IS... ME!

THE SUMMER

NO, I'M NOT SEEING ANY-ONE RIGHT NOW.

SORRY.

LIKE, REALLY POPULAR...

I BET YOU'RE REALLY POPULAR WITH THE GUYS, HUH?

WELL SHE SURE WASN'T ALONE **LAST** SUMMER...

I DON'T WANNA GO HOME

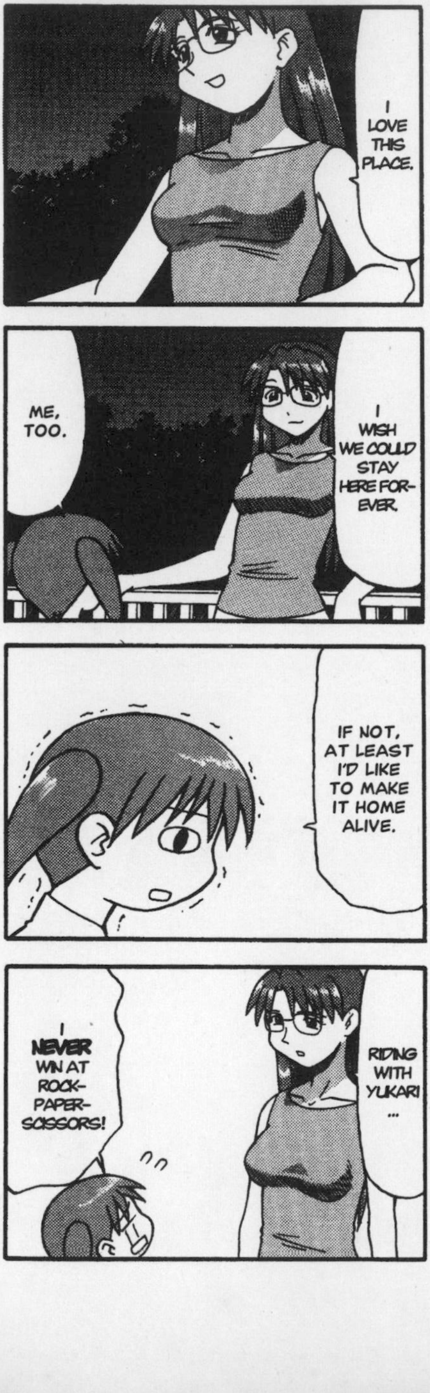
I LOVE THIS PLACE.
I WISH WE COULD STAY HERE FOREVER.
ME, TOO.
IF NOT, AT LEAST I'D LIKE TO MAKE IT HOME ALIVE.
RIDING WITH YUKARI ...
I NEVER WIN AT ROCK-PAPER-SCISSORS!

A LITTLE TOO INFORMAL

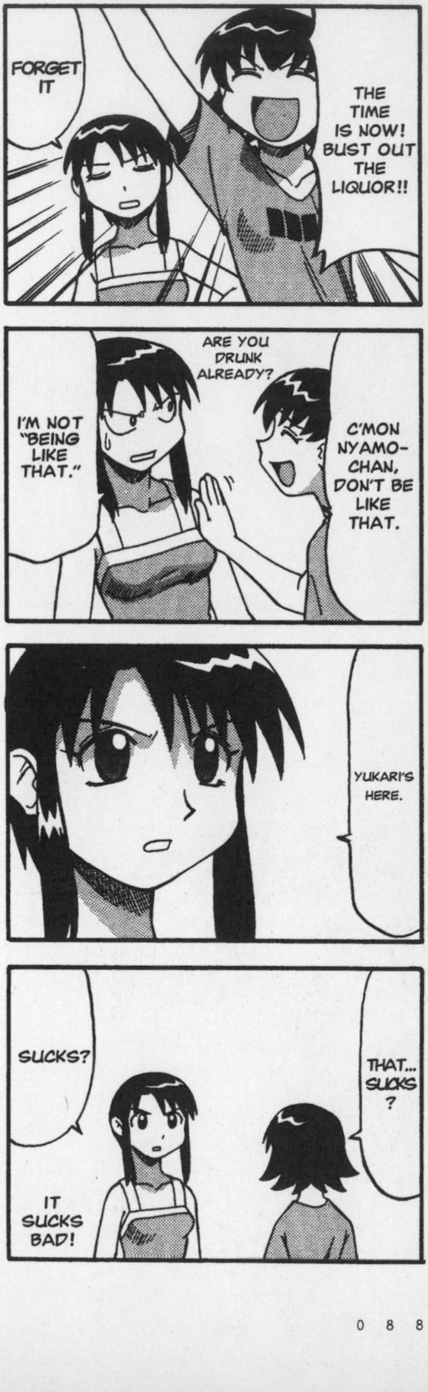
THE TIME IS NOW! BUST OUT THE LIQUOR!!
FORGET IT
C'MON NYAMO-CHAN, DON'T BE LIKE THAT.
I'M NOT "BEING LIKE THAT."
ARE YOU DRUNK ALREADY?
YUKARI'S HERE.
THAT... SUCKS?
SUCKS?
IT SUCKS BAD!

YOMI

EAT IT YOURSELF!

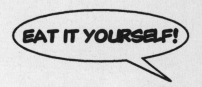

AARGH, I CAN'T TAKE IT!

EVERYONE'S BRAINS STILL WORKING AFTER THAT LONG SUMMER BREAK?

WOW! IT'S BEEN A WHILE, HUH?

'CAUSE YOU KNOW, MY BRAIN IS **TOTALLY** OUT TO LUNCH!

GOD, I'M ALREADY TIRED...

MOAN

I'LL DO IT!

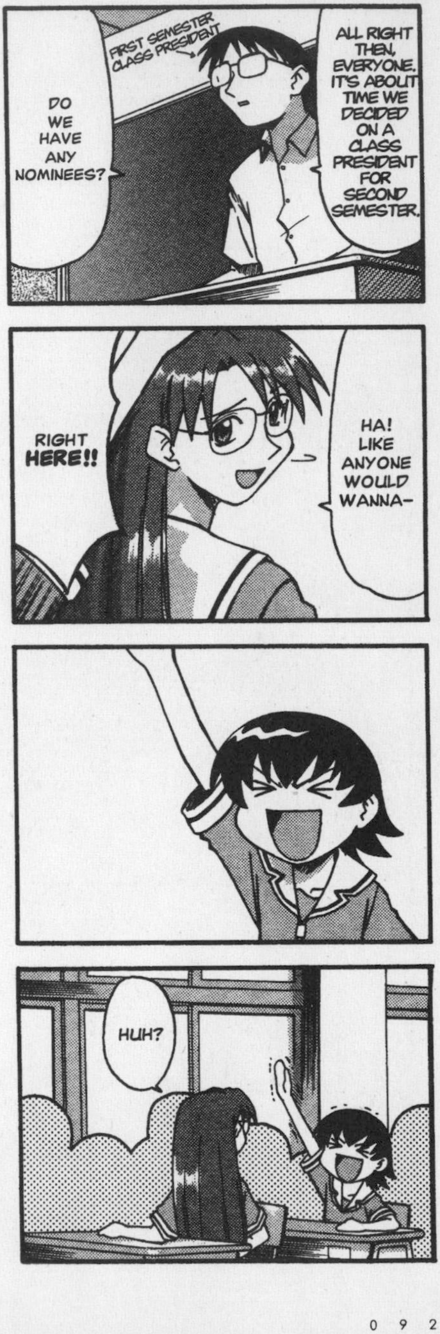
FIRST SEMESTER CLASS PRESIDENT
ALL RIGHT THEN, EVERYONE. IT'S ABOUT TIME WE DECIDED ON A CLASS PRESIDENT FOR SECOND SEMESTER.
DO WE HAVE ANY NOMINEES?
HA! LIKE ANYONE WOULD WANNA-
RIGHT **HERE!!**
HUH?

WHAT'D I MISS?

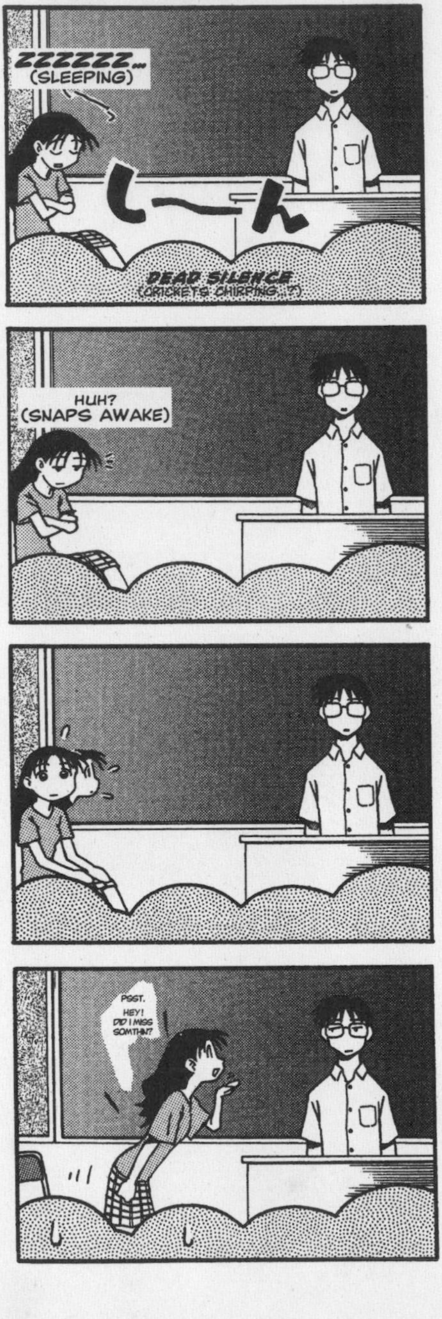
ZZZZZZ...
(SLEEPING)
しーん
DEAD SILENCE
(CRICKETS CHIRPING...?)
HUH?
(SNAPS AWAKE)
PSST.
HEY!
DID I MISS SOMTHIN'?

WHAT'S WITH YOU? YOU'RE ACTING LIKE IT'S A BAD THING I NOMINATED MYSELF.

HMMM.

WHY DO YOU ALL OF A SUDDEN...?

WELL WHO'S GONNA RUN THEN? YOU?

IT IS A BAD THING.

WHAT CAN I SAY? CALL IT A MISSION...

ANYONE ELSE PLANNING ON RUNNING FOR CLASS PRESIDENT?!

NO WAY.

AND IT WAS SO QUIET...

...OR THE FACT THAT NO ONE ELSE WAS RAISING THEIR HANDS.

TOMO AS CLASS PRESIDENT... KINDA GIVES YOU A BAD FEELING, HUH?

I DON'T REALLY CARE, AS LONG AS IT'S NOT ME.

YOUR CHANCE FOR WHAT?!

...I THOUGHT, NOW'S MY CHANCE!

THE TOMO/CHIYO WAR (PART 2)

REMEMBER THE MADNESS

OSAKA–AT IT AGAIN

WHAT ARE YOU DOING?

IZZAT SO? GOOD FOR YOU.

Y'KNOW HOW SOMETIMES YOU CAN SEE THE CRUD THAT GETS STUCK IN YOUR EYES? I'M JUST CHECKING IT OUT.

THE CHILD PRESIDENT

EEP!

FROZEN! (STIFFENING UP AND GETTING NERVOUS)

WELL CHIYO-CHAN, WHY DON'T YOU GIVE US A LITTLE SPEECH

I'M TEN YEARS OLD AND, UH...THANK YOU VERY MUCH!

UM...UH...

BOWING

BANG!

WE'RE BEHIND YA, CHIYO-CHAN!

YOU CAN DO IT!

C'MON, CHIYO-CHAN!

UUGH...

HOW DARE YOU!

OH MY GOD!

LOOKS LIKE I TOSS AND TURN IN MY SLEEP, HUH?

IT'S A LITTLE LATE FOR THAT NOW...

WHY GOD, WHY?!

IN ONE EAR...

SHOW ME! SHOW ME!

I WANNA SEE, TOO!

HEY, I BROUGHT SOME PICTURES FROM MY SUMMER VACATION.

THAT WAS THAT DAY I COULDN'T GO WITH YOU, HUH? MY CLUB HAD A TRIP THAT SAME DAY...

YUP.

WHAAT? SAKAKI WAS THERE?!

UH... YOUR CLUB?

WHY OH WHY DIDN'T I GO...?

FEAR

WHAT'S THIS? AN ACCI-DENT?
YEAH, THAT'S YUKARI'S CAR.
OH, I HEARD ABOUT THIS. IT WAS PRETTY BAD, HUH, CHIYO-CHAN?
CHIYO-CHAN?
SHAKE SHIVER
ぷる ぷる

LIFE

MISS YUKARI. PLEASE STOP. PLEASE STOP. WILL YOU PLEASE-
I'M SORRY. I'M SORRY. IT'S ALL OVER! I'M GONNA DIE!
AAAHH! GRANDPA. GRANDPA!
WATCH OUT!
CHIYO-CHAN! TURN AWAY FROM THE LIGHT!!

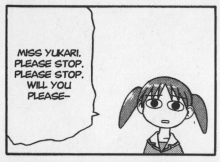

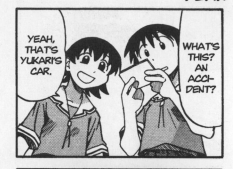

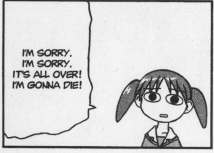

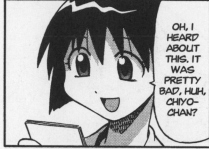

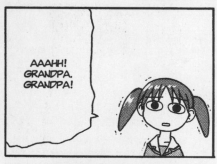

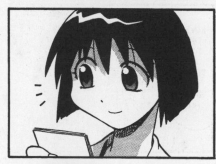

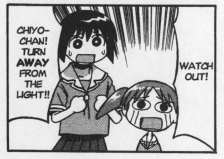

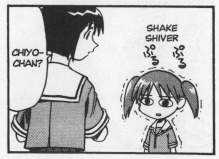

MUST BE NICE

A STRANGE MAN

THE SCREAM

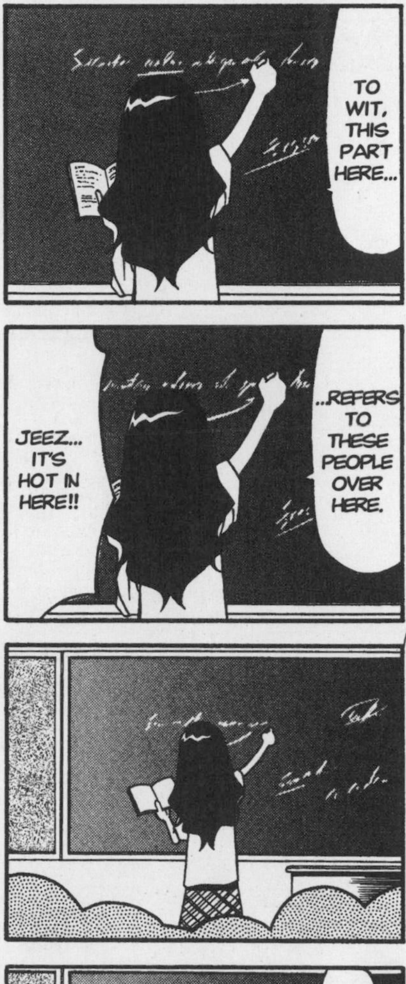
TO WIT, THIS PART HERE...
...REFERS TO THESE PEOPLE OVER HERE.
JEEZ... IT'S HOT IN HERE!!
FUR-THER-MORE...

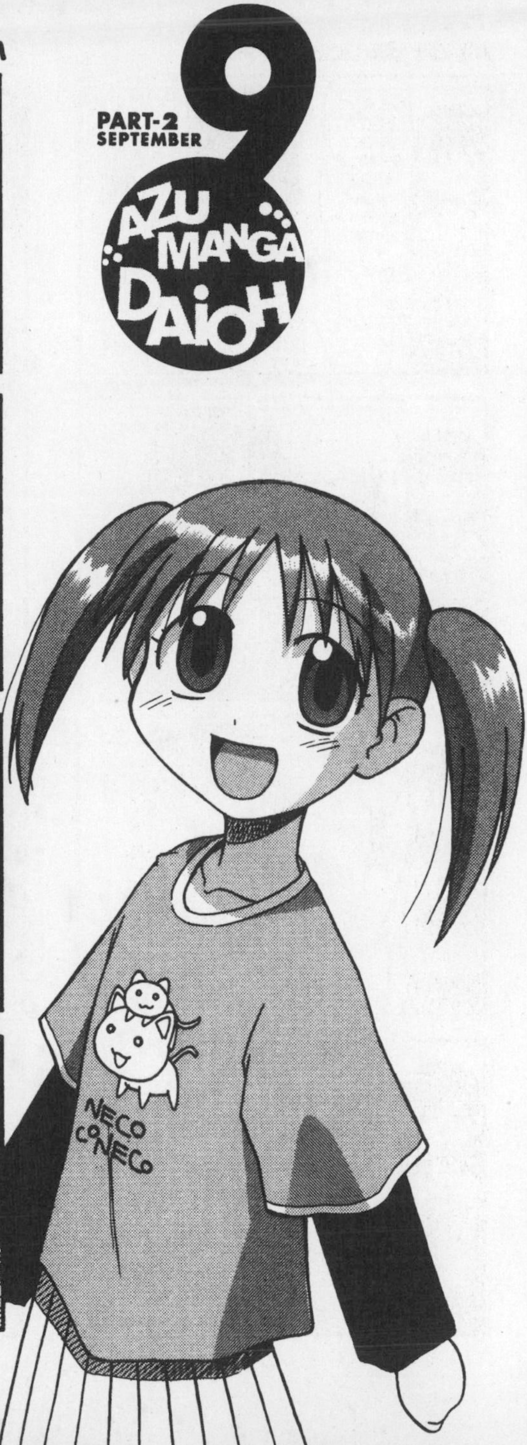
9
PART-2
SEPTEMBER
AZU MANGA DAIOH
NECO CONECO

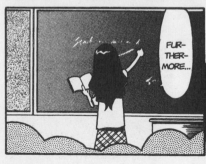

DANGEROUS

GEEZ, LOOK AT THAT RAIN! I WON'T BE ABLE TO GO HOME UNTIL IT STOPS.

RAINING CATS & DOGS

B- BUT IT LOOKS LIKE IT COULD START THUNDERING AT ANY—

I LOVE IT WHEN IT POURS DOWN LIKE THIS!

EEAAA!

KABOOM! (THUNDERCLAP)

YOU'RE THINKING OF AN EARTH- QUAKE.

QUICK, UNDER THE DESKS!

OHMAN OHMAN OHMAN...

SHE IS SO FREA- KING OUT...

COME ON A/C!!

MAN, IT'S HOT! I WISH THEY'D INSTALL A FRICKIN' AC IN OUR CLASS- ROOM.

THEY'VE GOT US OUTSIDE IN THE BLAZING HEAT.

YOU'RE LUCKY!

YEAH, WELL ANYWAY...

PANT

...I WISH THEY'D INSTALL A FRICKIN' A/C IN OUR CLASS- ROOM.

NO ESCAPE

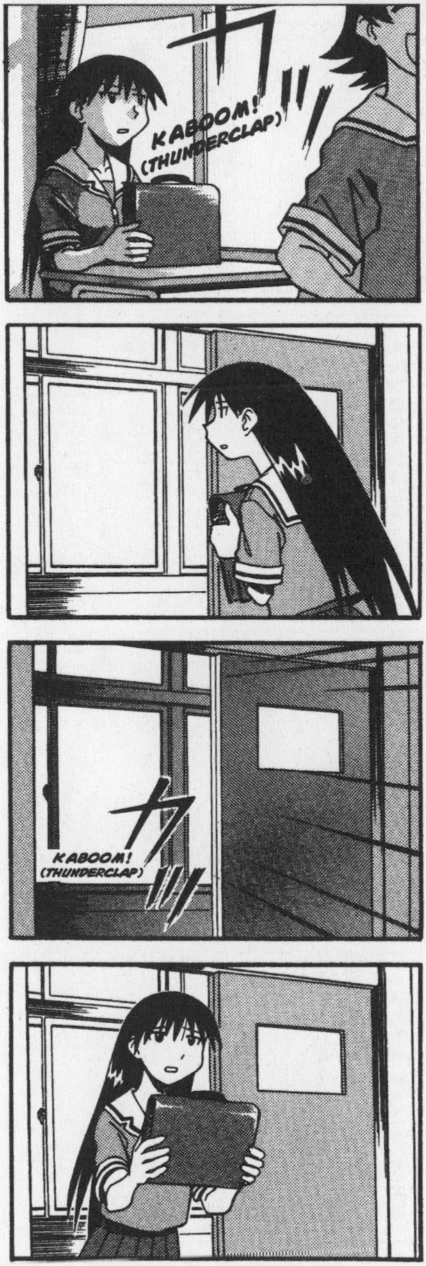
KABOOM!
(THUNDERCLAP)
KABOOM!
(THUNDERCLAP)

SCARY

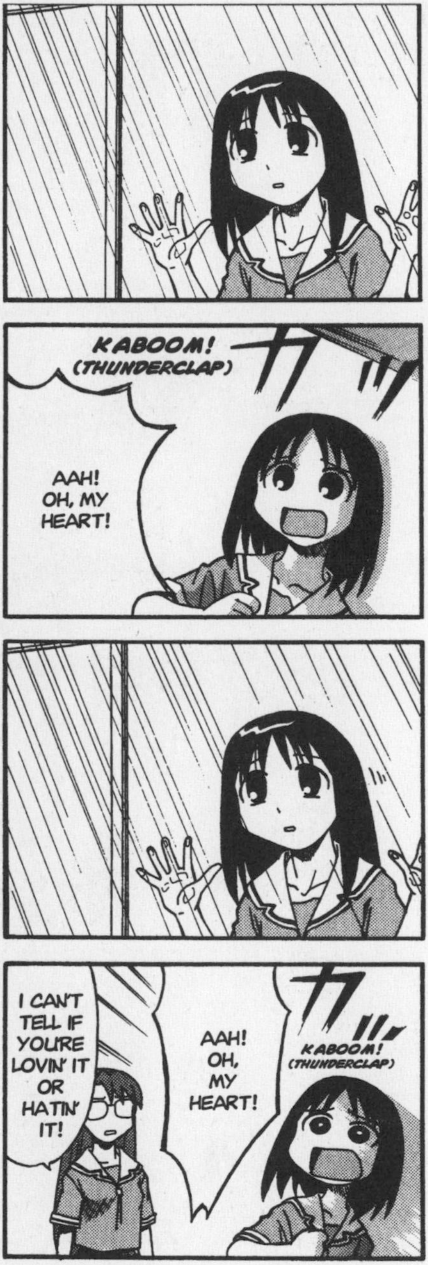
KABOOM!
(THUNDERCLAP)
AAH! OH, MY HEART!
KABOOM!
(THUNDERCLAP)
AAH! OH, MY HEART!
I CAN'T TELL IF YOU'RE LOVIN' IT OR HATIN' IT!

THE DEATH OF ME

HEY, YOU REMEMBER THAT OLD STORY ABOUT THE GOD OF LIGHTNING COMIN' DOWN TO STEAL YOUR BELLY BUTTON?
I DON'T GET IT.
IF HE TAKES IT, WHAT HAPPENS TO THAT PLACE WHERE YOUR BELLY BUTTON USED T'BE?
I DUNNO.
IT'D BE ALL RIGHT IF IT'S ALL SMOOTH, BUT WHAT IF IT JUST MAKES A BIG HOLE?
I'D FRICKIN' DIE!
I DONT THINK THAT'S SOMETHING YOU HAVE TO WORRY ABOUT...
KABOOM! (THUNDERCLAP)
AAH! OH, MY HEART!

WAAAH!

I SAW ON TV ONE TIME HOW THE INSIDE OF YOUR CAR IS SUPPOSED TO BE SAFE FROM LIGHTING.
WHAT YOU THINK? HUH, CHIYO-CHAN? ABOUT CARS?
C-CARS?
KABOOM! (THUNDERCLAP)
SO, WHADDYA THINK? CARS OR LIGHTNING, WHICH IS WORSE?
WAAAH! WAAAAH!!
HEY, LEAVE HER ALONE!

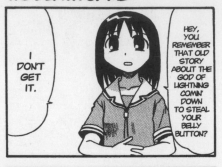

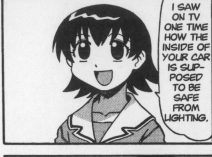

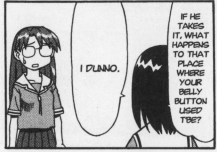

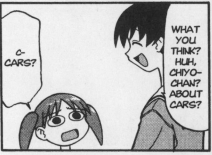

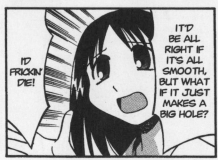

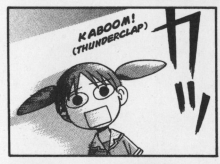

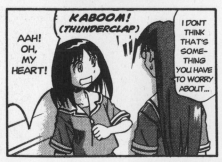

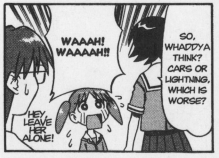

A MAN OF VALOR

I MEAN WE KNEW THE GUY WAS A PERV, BUT JUST SAYING IT LIKE THAT IN FRONT OF THE STUDENTS.

MAN, WHAT WAS UP WITH KIMURA LAST PERIOD...?

HUH?!

NO!!

TO STATE HIS TRUE FEELINGS SO HONESTLY, **RIGHT** TO THE STUDENTS...

WE, THE ENTIRE MALE STUDENT POPULATION, WERE DEEPLY MOVED!

I SHOULD HOPE NOT...

WE'VE NEVER HAD A TEACHER LIKE HIM BEFORE!

I LOVE MY JOB

CLASSICAL LITERATURE WITH MR. KIMURA

...WHICH IS WHY EVERYONE SHOULD THINK LONG AND HARD ABOUT WHAT THEY WANT TO DO WITH THEIR LIVES.

WHY DID **YOU** DECIDE TO BECOME A TEACHER, MR. KIMURA?

I LOVE 'EM!

FOR THE TEENAGE GIRLS!

BRRRRRRRING (SCHOOL BELL)

A QUESTION FOR THE TEACHER

YES'M?

MR. KIMURA?

YOU SAID YOU LIKE HIGH SCHOOL GIRLS, BUT WHAT ABOUT LITTLE CHIYO-CHAN OVER HERE?

MAKES SENSE.

HIGH SCHOOL IS HIGH SCHOOL!

ON THE PROWL

MISS KUROSAWA, MISS TANIZAKI

OH, I'M GOING OUT WITH MY FRIENDS LATER—

PERHAPS TODAY WE COULD ALL GO FOR A DRINK AFTER WORK.

AAH, THE BITTERNESS OF DEFEAT!

THE BITTERNESS OF...?

THAT GUY'S A LITTLE CREEPY.

THE PERFECT GENTLEMAN

THE WALK

OF COURSE! MR. TADAKICHI IS A PERFECT GENTLEMAN. THERE'S NOTHING TO BE AFRAID OF.

CA-CAN I PET HIM?

I'M TELLING YOU, IT'LL BE ALL RIGHT!

IF HE ENDS UP BITING ME, IT'S NOT GOING TO BE VERY FUNNY...

WHOSE DOG IS...?

SAKAKI

I TOLD YOU!

WHOA...

MR. TADK-ICHI...

HE'S OURS. HIS NAME IS MR. TADAKIC HI.

GIDDYUP!

A BIG DOG LIKE THIS... IT ALMOST LOOKS LIKE YOU COULD RIDE HIM.

I CAN RIDE HIM!

WELL, IT'S TIME FOR US TO BE GETTING ON WITH OUR WALK!

WHOA!

...A MR. TADAKICHI?

WHERE CAN I GET...

CLICK CLICK (DOG'S NAILS ON CONCRETE)

PAT PAT

PAT PAT

PAT PAT

PAT PAT

UM, WE SHOULD PPROBABLY BE GOING NOW...

PAT PAT

MISS KUROSAWA

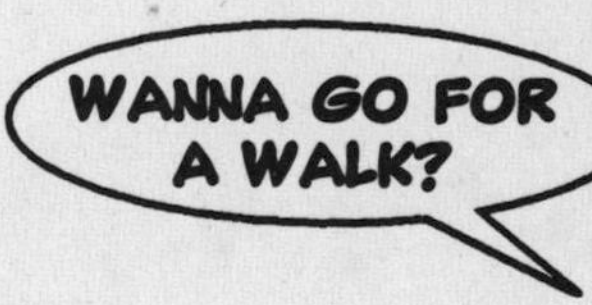
WANNA GO FOR A WALK?

WHICH REMINDS ME, I WENT TO GO SEE *RUNAWAY BRIDE* LAST NIGHT.

WELL, KINDA.

WHO'D YOU GO WITH? WAS IT A DATE?

MISS KUROSAWA SAID SHE SAW IT LAST NIGHT, TOO.

LET'S GET BACK TO THE LESSON.

THIS ISN'T THE TIME TO BE TALKING ABOUT MOVIES!

A QUESTION FOR THE TEACHER

THAT'S ALL FOR TODAY, CLASS.

キーンコーン

TAP TAP (FOLDER ON DESK)

BBBRRR RINGGG (SCHOOL BELL)

MA'AM?

WHAT'S THAT?

THERE WAS SOMETHING IN CLASS I DIDN'T UNDERSTAND A MINUTE AGO.

OH, SHUT UP!

YOU **DID** GO SEE THAT MOVIE WITH MISS KUROSAWA, DIDNCHYA?

JUMP CHIYO-CHAN, JUMP!

YES, MA'AM!

SKKRRRAA! (CHAIR SCOOTING AS SHE STANDS)

ガッ

OK, CHIYO-CHAN, WOULD YOU WRITE THIS IN ENGLISH, PLEASE?

STOP PICKING ON HER! LIKE YOU'RE GONNA LOOK AT IT ANY-WAY!

YOU'RE WRITING IT TOO LOW! I CAN'T SEE!

···

SORRY, CHIYO-CHAN. I DIDN'T MEAN FOR YOU TO HAVE TO JUMP...

SCRITCH SCRITCH (CHALK SCRAPING)

カッ カッ

BOUNCE BOUNCE

AGAIN?! WHY DON'T YOU TRY DOING IT YOURSELF SOMETIME?

HEY, WILL YOU SHOW ME YOUR MATH HOMEWORK?

JUST WHAT? AND STOP MAKING THAT FACE!

YOU'RE SO PRETTY, MISS YUKARI. IT'S JUST...

IN OTHER WORDS, YOU DIDN'T FEEL LIKE DOING IT.

IT'S NOT LIKE I DIDN'T **WANT** TO DO IT. I JUST DIDN'T HEAR WHAT THE ASSIGNMENT WAS.

YOU THINK SO?

I AGREE. SHE'S PRETTY UNTIL SHE STARTS TALKING!

FORGET IT. THER'D BE MISTAKES ALL OVER THE PLACE. I'LL DO IT MYSELF.

OK, HOW'S THIS? NEXT TIME, I'LL DO **YOUR** HOMEWORK FOR YOU.

HERE'S A CHOICE—DO IT YOUR DAMN SELF!

WELL THEN, I GUESS I HAVE NO CHOICE BUT TO LOOK AT YOURS...

YEAH, THAT'S ABOUT RIGHT.

HEY! ARE YOU SAYING ONCE I OPEN MY BIG YAP I'M NOT PRETTY ANYMORE?

FREE-FOR-ALL

HEH. YOU'RE PRETTY GOOD WITH THE JOKES, THERE.

SNAP! (ANGRY)

HOW MUCH CHUCK WOULD A WOODCHUCK WOOD IF A CHUCKWOOD WOULD CHUCK WOOD.

WELL, COME ON. TRY CRACKING A JOKE OR SOMETHING.

A WORD OF THANKS...?

GEEZ...

HERE.

WOOHOO!

HUH?

UH-UH. WHAT'S THE MAGIC WORD...?

YOU'RE THE ONE WHO'S STUPID!

THAT'S JUST STUPID.

HUH? WHAT ARE YOU TALKING ABOUT?

A LACK OF COMPREHENSION

KIMURA'S ASSERTION

NO EXCUSES

OK EVERYONE, TOMORROW IS THE SCHOOL SPORTS FESTIVAL.

SO YOU'D BETTER GIVE EVERYTHING YOU'VE GOT. GOT IT?

BLUE TEAM?

THAT'S MISS KURO-SAWA'S CLASS.

WE **MUST** DEFEAT BLUE TEAM AT ALL COSTS! THERE ARE **NO** EXCUSES!

DO WE EVEN **HAVE** ANY MEANS?

BY ANY AND ALL MEANS NECES-SARY!!

MISS FORGETFULNESS

WHERE'S MY...?

SURE.

HEY, CAN I BORROW A PEN? I FORGOT MINE.

OSAKA, YOU'RE ALWAYS FORGETTING STUFF, HUH?

ACTUALLY, I WOULD.

YEAH... YOU WOULDN'T THINK SO, BUT...

A DECLARATION OF WAR

THE VICTORY EQUATION

KAGURA VS. SAKAKI

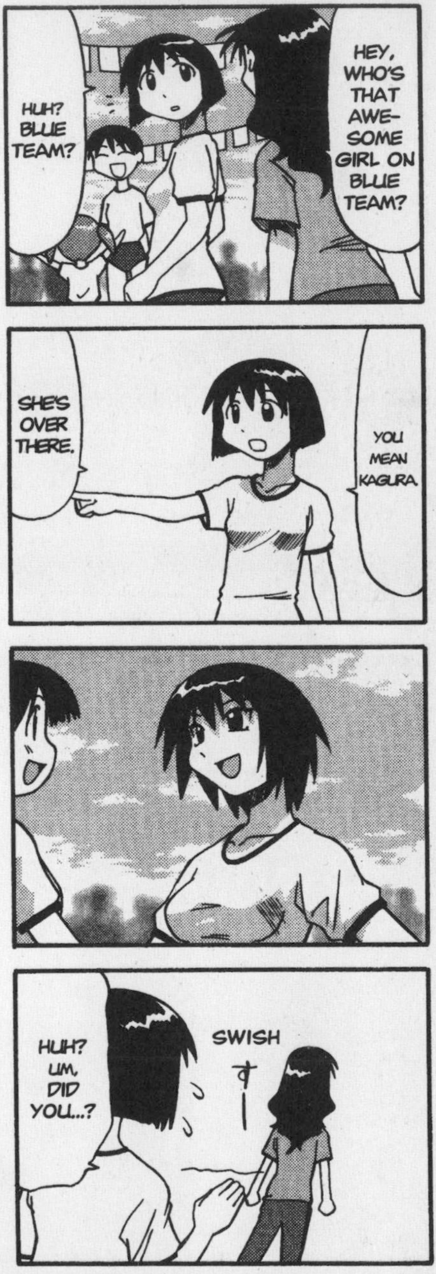
HEY, WHO'S THAT AWE-SOME GIRL ON BLUE TEAM?
HUH? BLUE TEAM?
YOU MEAN KAGURA.
SHE'S OVER THERE.
SWISH
すー
HUH? UM, DID YOU...?

THE SETUP

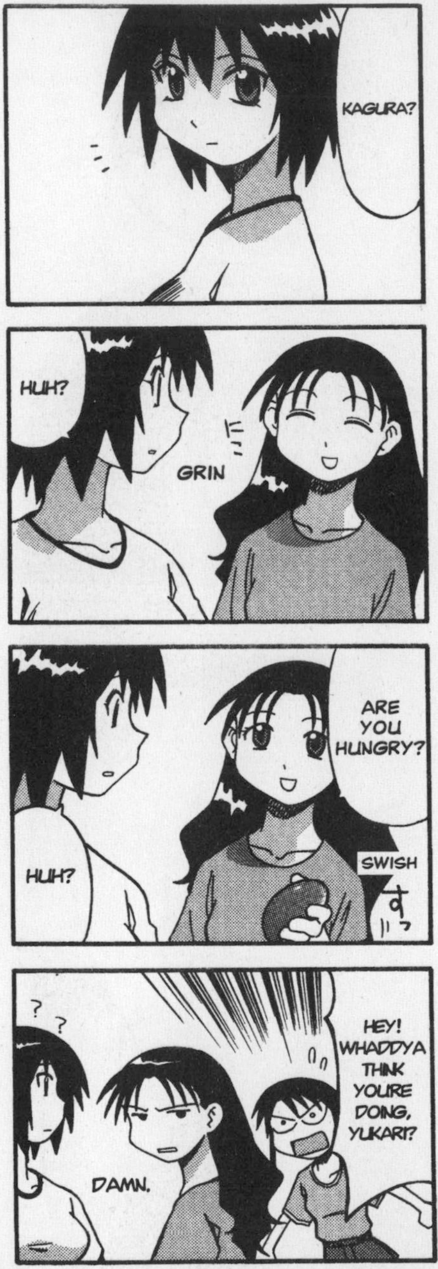
KAGURA?
HUH?
GRIN
ARE YOU HUNGRY?
SWISH
すっ
HUH?
HEY! WHADDYA THINK YOU'RE DOING, YUKARI?
DAMN.

GOOD LUCK AND I'M SORRY

ALL RIGHT! LET'S DO IT!

MADAM PRESIDENT! A FEW WORDS TO RALLY THE TROOPS!

HUH?

B- BUT I DON'T WANNA BE THE ONE HOLDING EVERY-ONE BACK.

UH, ALL RIGHT. UMM... GOOD LUCK, EVERY-ONE!

TAKE IT EASY! IT'S ONLY A SPORTS FESTIVAL.

SOB SOB

IF WE LOSE BECAUSE OF ME...

IT'S ALL RIGHT

BURNING TO WIN

THAT GIRL'S LIKE LIGHTNING!

400 METER DASH

YEAH, SHE EVEN CAME IN FIRST IN THE 100 METER DASH.

GO SAKAKI!

WHOAA, LOOK AT 'ER GO! THAT GIRL'S LIKE LIGHTNING!

EEEW!

BUT HER SHIRT ISN'T TUCKED INTO HER SHORTS!!

SHUT UP! SHUT UP!!

AND YOU! INTO THE SHORTS!

ONE...ONE...ONE...

WISH US LUCK!

THREE-LEGGED RACE

ばた
FLOP

YEAH, OK. SLOWLY...

ON THE COUNT OF THREE, LET'S GET UP TOGETHER.

ばた
FLOP

ONE!

CAN'T LET GO

HEAVE **HO!** HEAVE **HO!**

CHIYO-CHAN AT THE TAIL END

UUUGH...

WAAAH...

SLIDE SLIDE SLIDE

PULL, OSAKA!

HEAVE HO!

TUG-OF-WAR

I WONDER WHAT "HO" MEANS...

HEAVE HO!

HEAVE HO! HEAVE HO!

HEAVE HO!

SHUT UP AND PULL!

WHAT DOES "HO" MEAN?!

OSAKA WITH GLASSES

LET'S TRY IT!

TURN, TURN, HOP, HOP

YOU AGAIN?

THE MOMENT

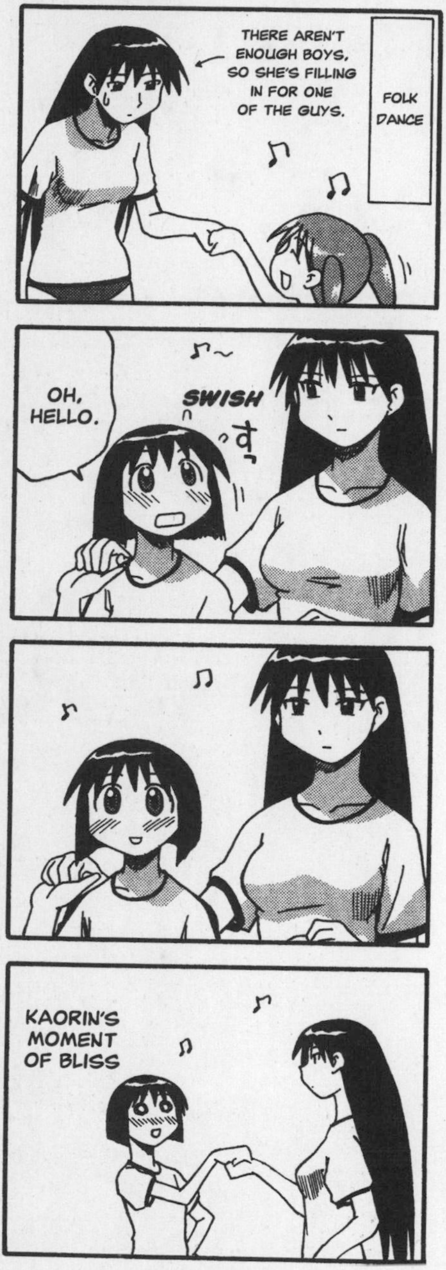

FOLK DANCE
THERE AREN'T ENOUGH BOYS, SO SHE'S FILLING IN FOR ONE OF THE GUYS.
OH, HELLO.
SWISH
KAORIN'S MOMENT OF BLISS

WOO-HOO!

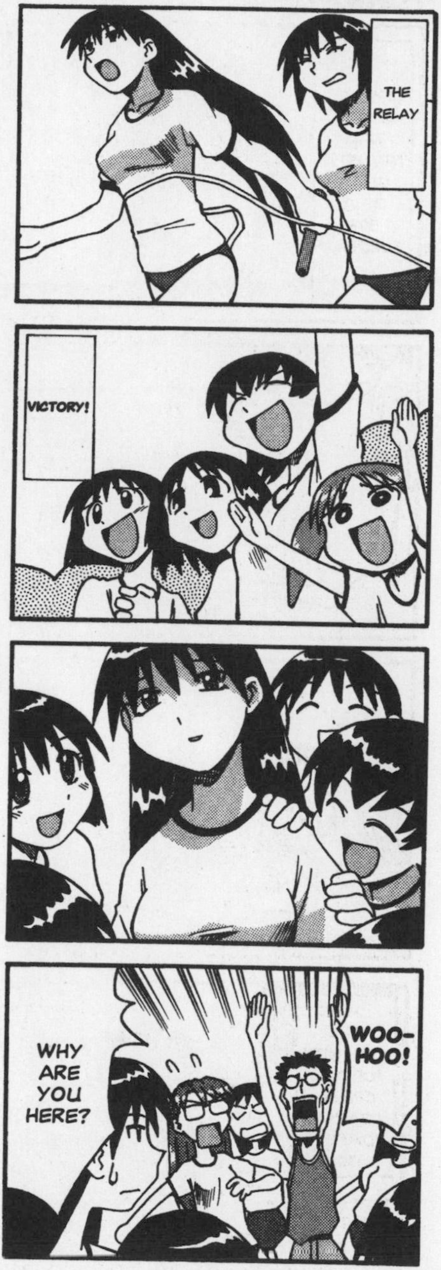

THE RELAY
VICTORY!
WHY ARE YOU HERE?
WOO-HOO!

HELLO AND GOODBYE

WELCOME!

KAORIN

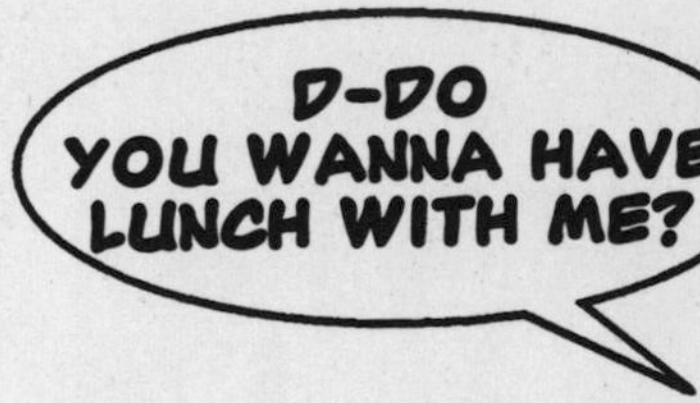
D-DO YOU WANNA HAVE LUNCH WITH ME?

I KNEW IT

AZU MANGA DAIOH

NOVEMBER PART-1

FLIP ぴょこ

DON'T YOU DARE FALL SLEEP WHILE I'M WORKING.

SHE WOULD DO IT FOR REAL

WE MADE IT TO THE ROOF.

WHAT BEAUTIFUL WEATHER—THE WIND FEELS SO GOOD!

I BET I COULD FLY LIKE A BIRD IF I JUMPED OFF THIS BUILDING...

JUST CHECKING

IT WAS THIS BIG AND...AND...

JIGGLE JIGGLE

SO, UH, HOW BIG WAS IT, THEN?

CAN I HELP YOU?

GIMME GIMME

WHAT?

WOW, THAT LOOKS GOOD. CAN I HAVE A BITE?

DON'T I ALWAYS LET YOU COPY MY HOMEWORK?

YOU WISH!

THAT'S MY LINE!

DON'T EVEN TRY IT...

IT'S NICE EATING LUNCH UP HERE ON THE ROOF, ISN'T IT?

YEAH, THE HIGHER YOU ARE, THE BETTER THE FOOD TASTES.

もぐ もぐ MUNCH MUNCH

IT'S LIKE THIS

THANKS, THAT WAS GOOD

GOOD LUCK

DIGGIN' YOUR OWN GRAVE

IT WASN'T ME

WELL, LET'S SEE EVERY-ONE'S SUG-GES-TIONS.

LET'S RETHINK WHAT WE SHOULD DO FOR THE CULTURAL FESTIVAL.

CLANK ZING (COIN BOUNCING OFF DESK)

OSAKA'S SUGGESTION

SOME THING... INTER-ESTING...

A HAUNTED HOUSE ISN'T ALL THAT INTER-ESTING, EITHER.

WHAT THE HELL ARE YOU THINK-ING?

WHY DON'T WE HAVE A SPORTS FESTIVAL INSTEAD?

BUNNY UNIFORM

STUFFED WONDERLAND

DOLLING THEM UP

THE CUTE MASCOT

MASCOT

AZU MANGA DAIOH

NOVEMBER PART-2

STUFFED
YEAH! TEAM YUKARI!

SAKAKI

ネコ係
CAT DIVISION

THE DAY OF THE SCHOOL FESTIVAL

YEAH. THEY REALLY TURNED OUT GREAT.

W-WOW! THIS TURNED OUT PRETTY GOOD, TOO.

LET ME TRY IT ON. BUT YOU'RE NOT WEARING IT RIGHT.

...NOT WEARING IT RIGHT...?

A FRIEND?

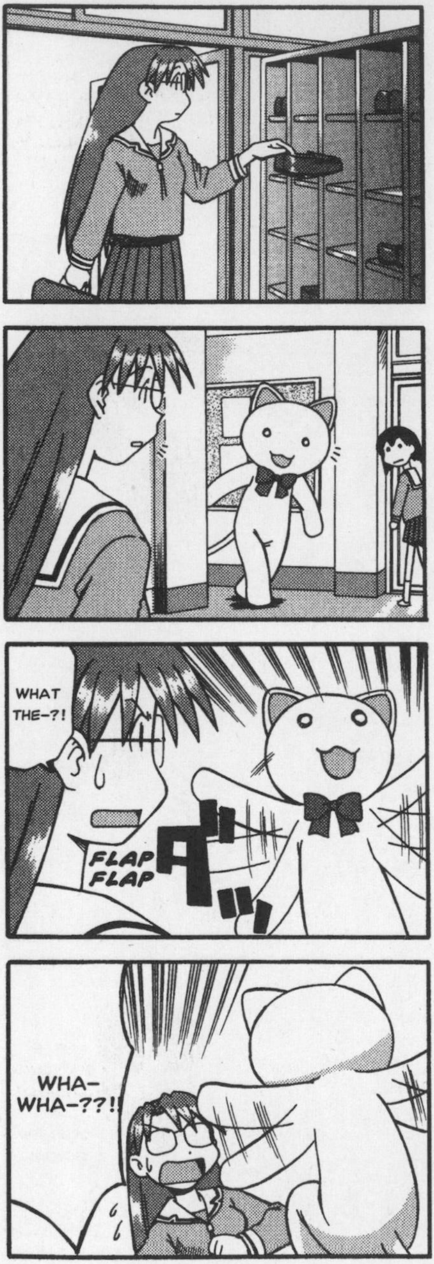
WHAT THE–?!
FLAP FLAP
WHA–
WHA–??!!

HYPED!

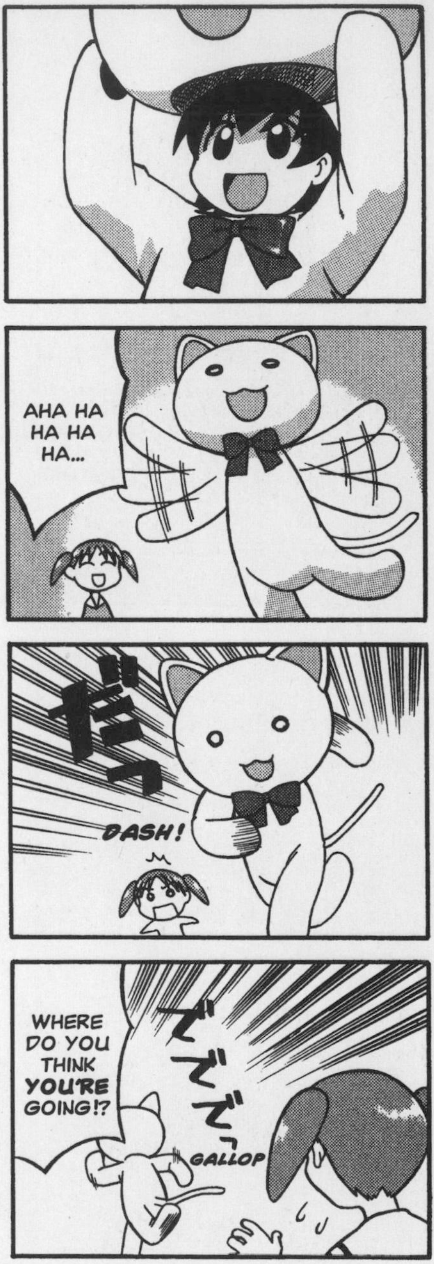
AHA HA
HA HA
HA...
DASH!
WHERE DO YOU THINK YOU'RE GOING!?
GALLOP

A MYSTERIOUS CREATURE

I'M BACK

TASTY WATER

FINE. FORGET ABOUT THE SWIMSUIT.

JUST GIMME A GLASS OF POOL WATER.

WHAT?

GROAN...

ARE YOU OUT OF YOUR MIND?!

POOL WATER! THE WATER THAT ALL YOU GIRLS HAVE BEEN SOAKING IN!

THE WRONG IDEA

DRINK

-TO BENEFIT THE SWIM CLUB

WELL...

HOW'RE SALES?

WHY IS NO ONE WEARING A SWIMSUIT! YOU **ARE** IN THE SWIM CLUB, AREN'T YOU?!

OH DEAR...

HEY, MISS KUROSAWA, GOOD TIMING! PLEASE SAY SOMETHING!

A GOOD TEACHER?

HI, EVERY-ONE! I HOPE YOU'RE ALL DOING OK! GREAT!

OH, PERFECT TIMING!

A F-FOR-EIGNER!

WHERE ARE YOU GOING?!

DASH!
(RUNNING OFF IN A HURRY)

QUE?

WELCOME! PLEASE ENJOY YOURSELF!

OH! A FOR-EIGNER!

HALLO, MÄDCHEN, WIE GEHT ES DIR? WAS SIND DEINE ARHEN?

STUFFED WONDERLAND, TEAM YUKARI

ODER SIND DEINE ARHE NATURAL? DU BIST SEHR SCHÖN!

QUE?

STUFFED WONDERLAND, TEAM YUKARI

REQUESTED BY TOMO

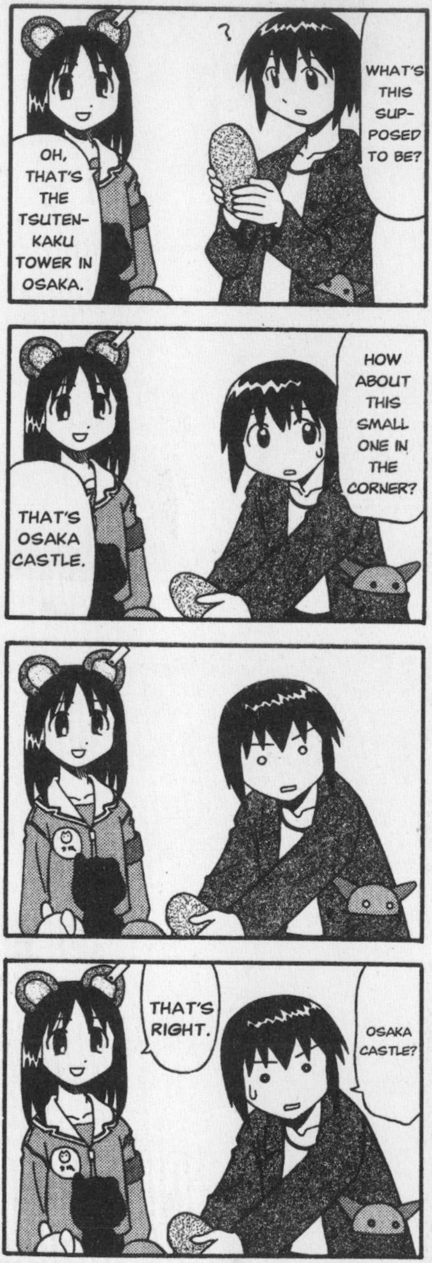
?
WHAT'S THIS SUP-POSED TO BE?
OH, THAT'S THE TSUTEN-KAKU TOWER IN OSAKA.
HOW ABOUT THIS SMALL ONE IN THE CORNER?
THAT'S OSAKA CASTLE.
THAT'S RIGHT.
OSAKA CASTLE?

I MADE IT

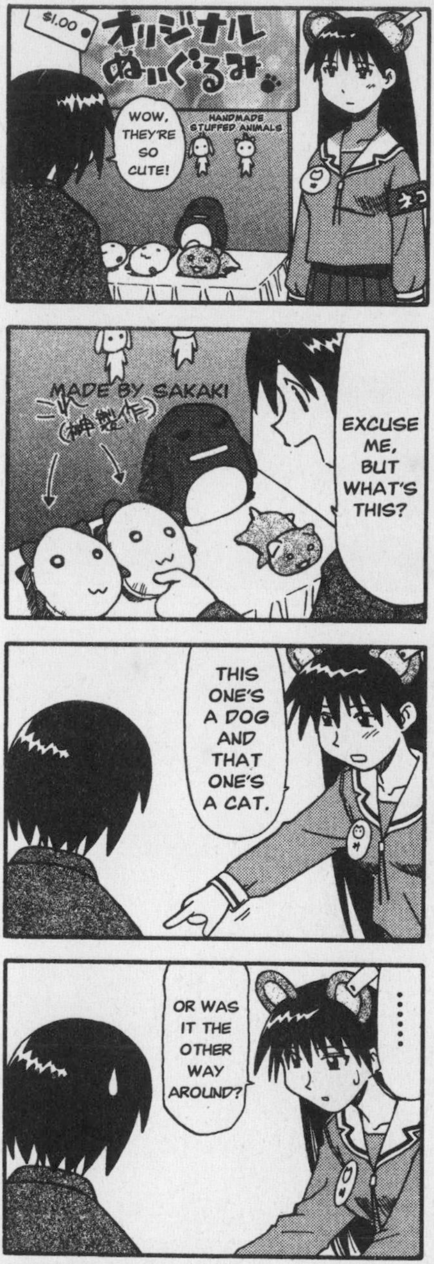
$1.00
オリジナル
ぬいぐるみ
HANDMADE STUFFED ANIMALS
WOW, THEY'RE SO CUTE!
MADE BY SAKAKI
EXCUSE ME, BUT WHAT'S THIS?
THIS ONE'S A DOG AND THAT ONE'S A CAT.
OR WAS IT THE OTHER WAY AROUND?
......

A SURPRISE INSIDE

THE PERFECT OPPORTUNITY

INTRUDER?

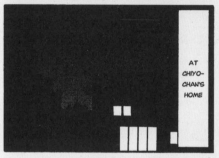

AT CHIYO-CHAN'S HOME

WOOF! WOOF! WOOF!!

FROM THE FESTIVAL

MR. TADAKICHI!

WOOF! WOOF! WOOF!!

IT'S TIME TO...

THE FESTIVAL WAS A BIG SUCCESS!

GREAT JOB EVERY-ONE!

WELL, LET'S TAKE THESE STUFFED ANIMALS AND..

WHAAAT?

...BURN THEM ALL!

FOR WHAT?

AREN'T WE SUPPOSED TO HAVE A MEMORIAL SERVICE?

MR. TADAKICHI

AZU MANGA DAIOH 2

TERRIBLY SORRY

CHIYO-CHAN'S PANDA

I DIDN'T KNOW THAT

JUST FOR A CHANGE

OSAKA'S PANDA

I AM PELÉ

YUKARI OF THE WIND

GO--AL!

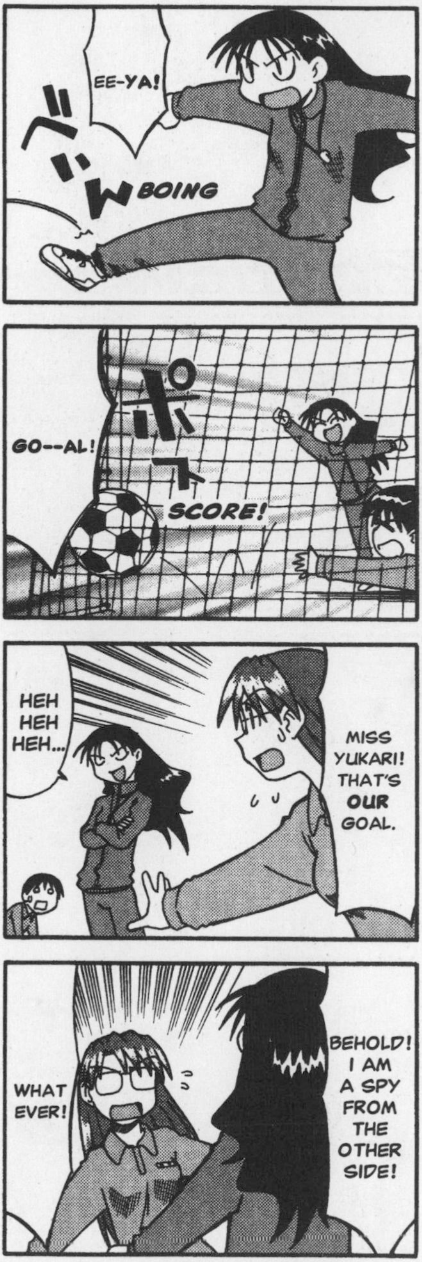

EE-YA!
BOING
GO--AL!
SCORE!
HEH HEH HEH...
MISS YUKARI! THAT'S OUR GOAL.
BEHOLD! I AM A SPY FROM THE OTHER SIDE!
WHAT EVER!

I TOLD YOU I'M PELÉ!

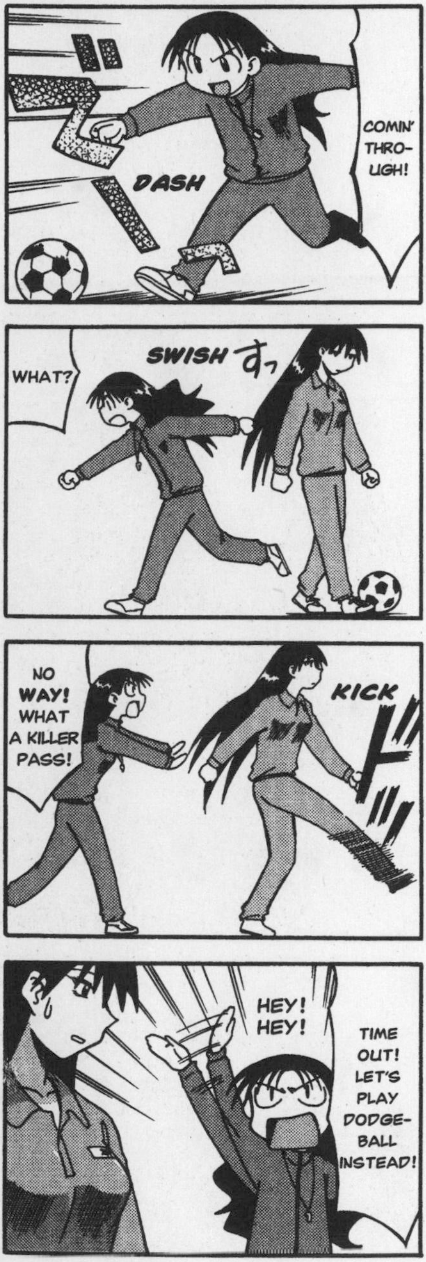

COMIN' THRO-UGH!
DASH
SWISH すっ
WHAT?
KICK
NO WAY! WHAT A KILLER PASS!
HEY! HEY!
TIME OUT! LET'S PLAY DODGE-BALL INSTEAD!

LEFT AND RIGHT

FOR SOME REASON, CHIYO-CHAN IS THE LAST ONE LEFT.

JUST HIT HER ALREADY.

HERE IT COMES!

RUN, CHIYO-CHAN

YA!

CATCH

KICK THEIR BUTTS!!

OH MY GOD!

BONK!

VACATION PLANS

OUT OF ORDER

DYING TO SEE IT

THAT'S A GREAT IDEA!

WHY DON'T WE ALL GO TO THE ZOO TO SEE SOME REAL PANDAS?

WHAT'S THAT?

YEAH, BUT THERE'S SOMETHING ELSE I WANNA SEE.

UHHH...

WHAT WAS THE NAME OF THAT THING...?

WELL, GOOD LUCK.

OH, YEAH. THE CHUPACABRA.

I BOUGHT IT

THE PANDA BOOK?

LOOK WHAT I BOUGHT.

OOOH, CHECK 'EM OUT.

THEY'RE ADORABLE!

REALLY? THEY'RE SOOO CUTE!

YOU KNOW, I NEVER SEEN A REAL PANDA BEFORE.

UHHHH...

IS IT BLACK ON WHITE OR WHITE ON BLACK?

SOMETHING SPECIAL

DECEMBER
PART-2

LEMME SEE.

I GOT THESE AS A CHRIST-MAS GIFT.

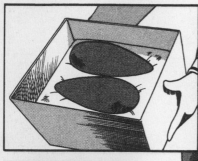

AND, UH... WHAT ARE THEY?

+++

OPINION

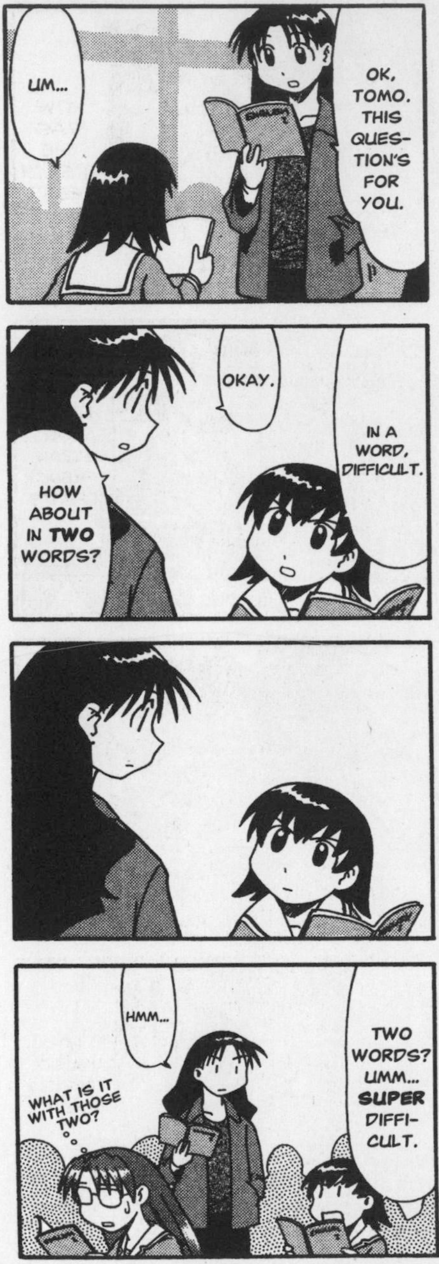
UM...
OK, TOMO. THIS QUES-TION'S FOR YOU.
OKAY.
IN A WORD, DIFFICULT.
HOW ABOUT IN TWO WORDS?
HMM...
TWO WORDS? UMM... SUPER DIFFI-CULT.
WHAT IS IT WITH THOSE TWO?

NEW ONES

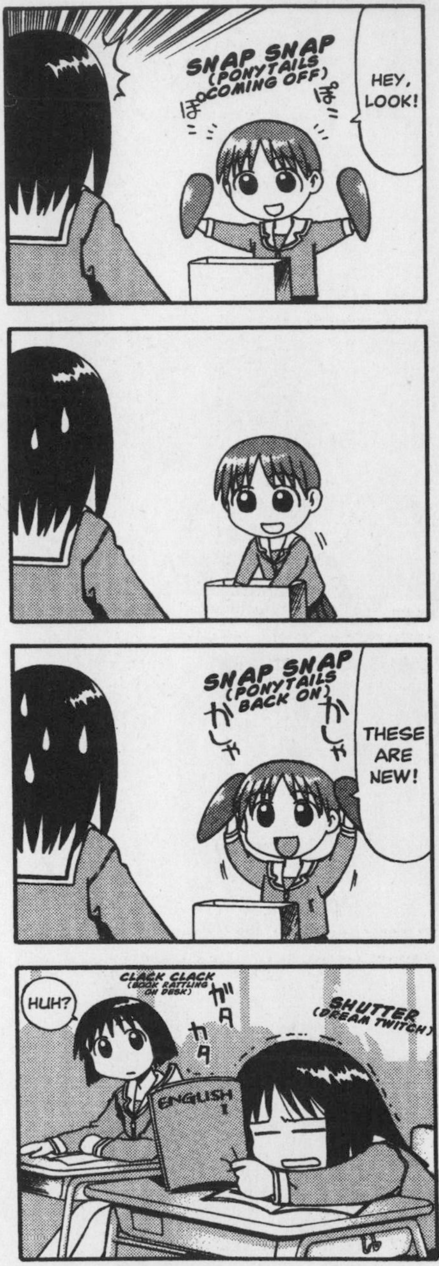
SNAP SNAP (PONYTAILS COMING OFF)
ぽ ぽ
HEY, LOOK!
SNAP SNAP (PONYTAILS BACK ON)
かしゃ かしゃ
THESE ARE NEW!
CLACK CLACK (BOOK RATTLING ON DESK)
HUH?
SHUTTER (DREAM TWITCH)
ENGLISH 1

PRETEND IT DIDN'T HAPPEN

DIDN'T MEAN TO DO IT

REPORT CARD

I HAVE EVERY-ONE'S REPORT CARDS HERE.

YES?

CHIYO-CHAN!

WHOA...

YOU'RE ONE OF THE TOP STUDENTS IN THE SCHOOL!

NEXT.

WHAT YOU LEARN HERE WON'T HELP YOU AFTER GRADUATION, THOUGH.

PATHETIC

CLEAN-ING DAY

SWEEP SWEEP

...I FEEL SO PATHETIC, LIKE I CAN'T DO ANYTHING.

WHEN I SEE YOU ALL WORKING SO HARD...

SIGH

SO WHY DON'T YOU GET TO WORK?

CHRISTMAS PARTY

EDUCATION

NO MERCY

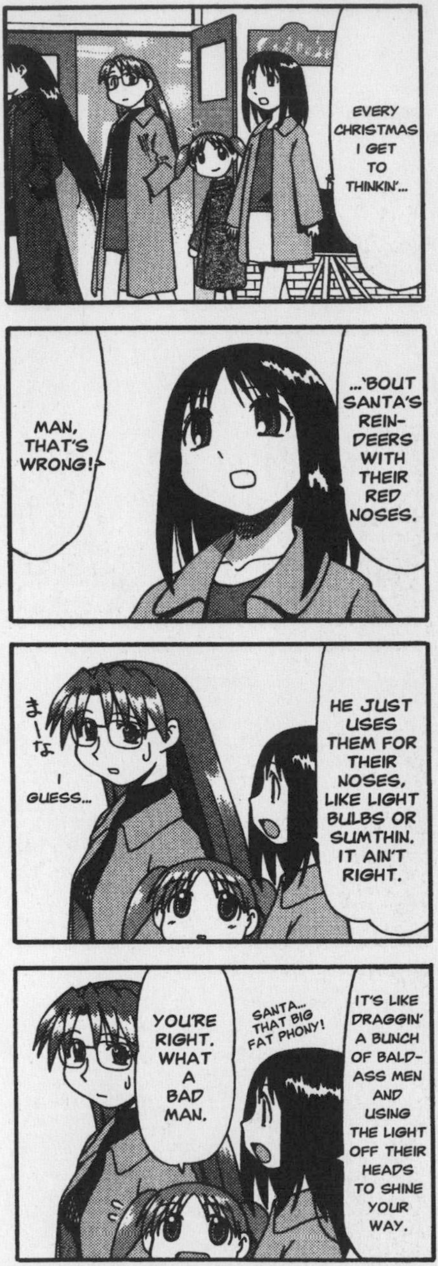

EVERY CHRISTMAS I GET TO THINKIN'...
...'BOUT SANTA'S REIN-DEERS WITH THEIR RED NOSES.
MAN, THAT'S WRONG!
HE JUST USES THEM FOR THEIR NOSES, LIKE LIGHT BULBS OR SUMTHIN. IT AIN'T RIGHT.
まーな
I GUESS...
IT'S LIKE DRAGGIN' A BUNCH OF BALD-ASS MEN AND USING THE LIGHT OFF THEIR HEADS TO SHINE YOUR WAY.
SANTA... THAT BIG FAT PHONY!
YOU'RE RIGHT. WHAT A BAD MAN.

PHONY!

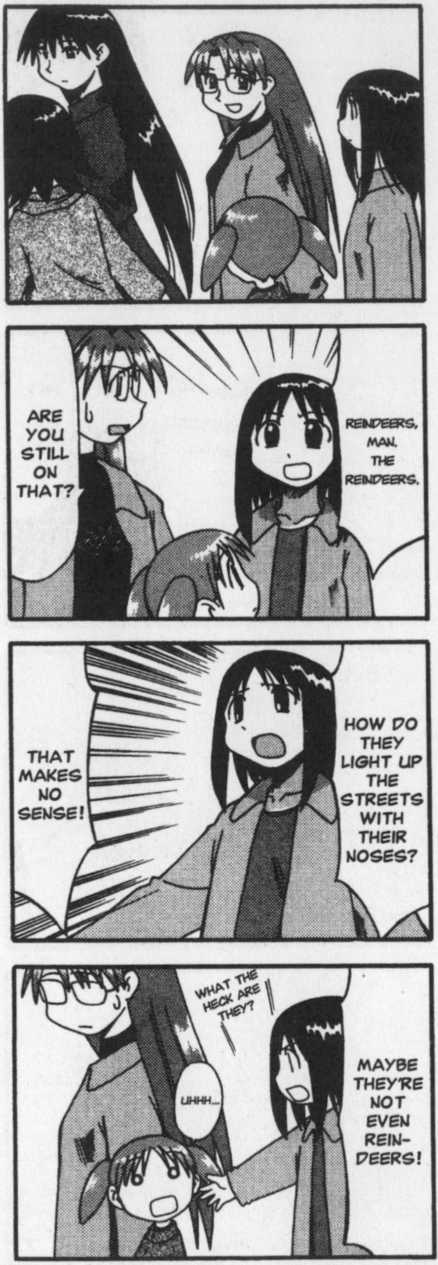

REINDEERS, MAN. THE REINDEERS.
ARE YOU STILL ON THAT?
HOW DO THEY LIGHT UP THE STREETS WITH THEIR NOSES?
THAT MAKES NO SENSE!
MAYBE THEY'RE NOT EVEN REIN-DEERS!
WHAT THE HECK ARE THEY?
UHHH...

GIVING IT EVERYTHING SHE'S GOT!

THE WILL TO WIN

WHOA.

BUT ONE OF US KINDA SUCKED...

AAH, SHUT IT! AT LEAST I SING FROM THE HEART!

YEAH! I THOUGHT YOU WAS CELINE DION OR SOMETHING.

I CAN'T BELIEVE YOU'RE SUCH A GREAT SINGER!

MAN, I SANG A **TON** OF SONGS.

A WHITE CHRISTMAS INDEED...

SNOWING ON CHRISTMAS! HOW ROMANTIC!

SNOW!

HOW THE HELL DID **YOU** GET HERE?

WHAT THE-?!

THE END

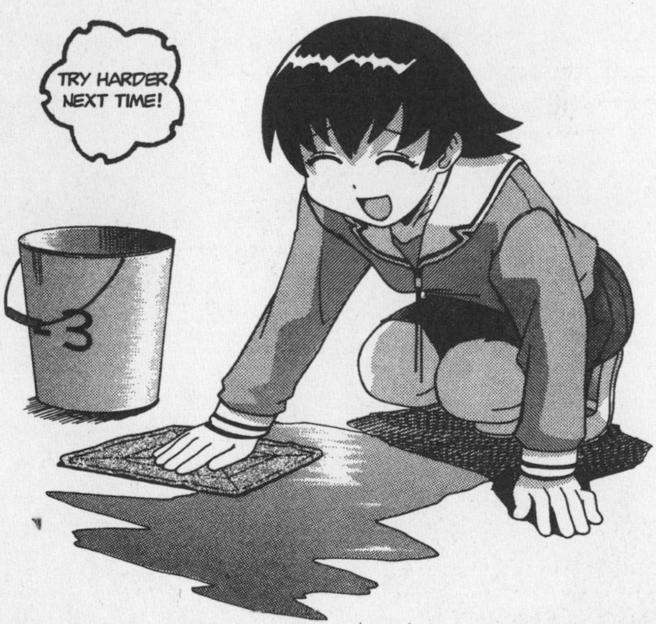
TRY HARDER NEXT TIME!

AZUMANGA DAIOH CHARACTERS

MR. TADAKICHI

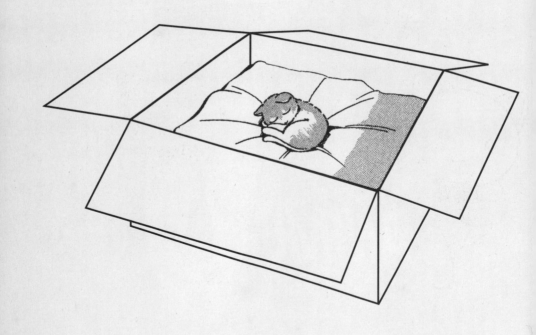

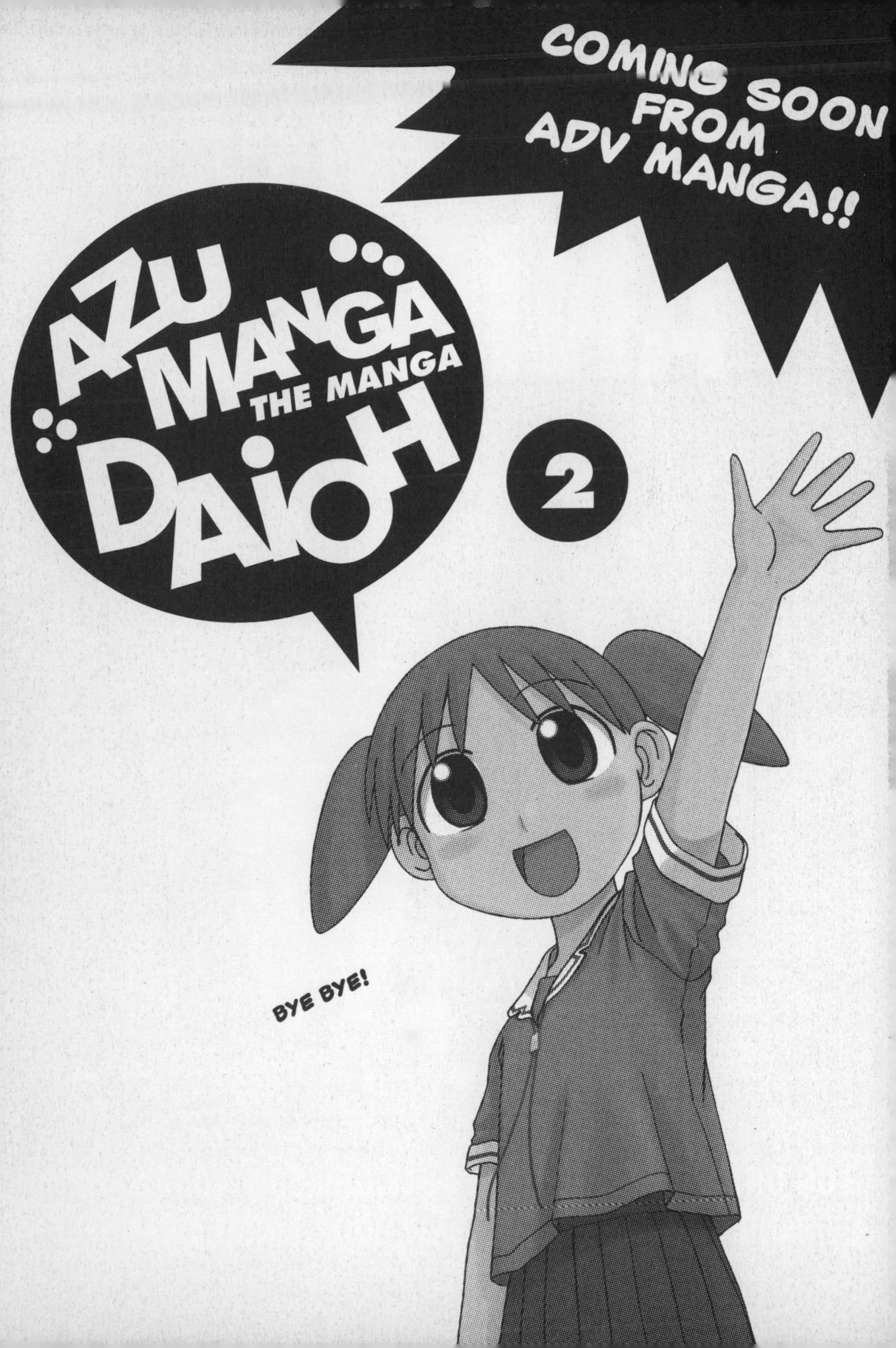
COMING SOON FROM ADV MANGA!!
AZUMANGA DAIOH
THE MANGA
2
BYE BYE!

Azumanga Daioh Volume one

© KIYOHIKO AZUMA 2000
Originally published in 2000 by MEDIA WORKS, Inc., Tokyo, Japan.

English translation rights arranged with MEDIA WORKS, Inc.

Translator **KAY BERTRAND**
Graphic Design **TAWNA FRANZE & WINDI MARTIN**
Logo Design **FUMIKO CHINO**
Graphic Artist **WINDI MARTIN**

Publishing Editor **SUSAN ITIN**

President, C.E.O. & Publisher **JOHN LEDFORD**

Email: editor@adv-manga.com
www.adv-manga.com
www.advfilms.com

For sales and distribution inquiries please call 1.800.282.7202

ADV MANGA is a division of A.D. Vision, Inc.
10114 W. Sam Houston Parkway, Suite 200, Houston, Texas 77099

English Edition
Produced by A.D. Vision, Inc. under exclusive license.
ADV MANGA is a trademark of A.D. Vision, Inc.

ISBN: 1-4139-0000-3

First printing, August 2003

10 9 8 7 6 5 4 3 2 1
Printed in Canada

ANIME SURVEY
FILL IT OUT AND YOU COULD WIN FABULOUS PRIZES!

PLEASE MAIL THE COMPLETED FORM TO: EDITOR – ADV MANGA
℅ A.D. Vision, Inc. 10114 W. Sam Houston Pkwy., Suite 200 Houston, TX 77099

Name: _____

Address: _____

City: State: Zip: _____

E-Mail: _____

Male ☐   Female ☐   Age: _____

Cable Provider: _____

☐ **CHECK HERE IF YOU WOULD LIKE TO RECEIVE OTHER INFORMATION OR FUTURE OFFERS FROM ADV.**

1. Annual Household Income (*check only one*)
  Under $25,000
  ☐ $25,000 to $50,000
  ☐ $50,000 to $75,000
  ☐ Over $75,000

2. How do you hear about new Anime releases? (*Check all that apply*)
  ☐ Browsing in Store   ☐ Magazine Ad
  ☐ Internet Reviews   ☐ Online Advertising
  ☐ Anime News Websites   ☐ Conventions
  ☐ Direct Email Campaigns   ☐ TV Advertising
  ☐ Online forums (message boards and chat rooms)
  ☐ Carrier pigeon
  ☐ Other:_____

3. Which magazines do you read? (*Check all that apply*)
  ☐ Wizard   ☐ YRB
  ☐ SPIN   ☐ EGM
  ☐ Animerica   ☐ Newtype USA
  ☐ Rolling Stone   ☐ SciFi
  ☐ Maxim   ☐ Starlog
  ☐ DC Comics   ☐ Wired
  ☐ URB   ☐ Vice
  ☐ Polygon   ☐ BPM
  ☐ Original Play Station Magazine   ☐ I hate reading
  ☐ Entertainment Weekly   ☐ Other:

4. Would you subscribe to digital cable if you could get a 24 hour/7 day a week anime channel (like the Anime Network)?
  ☐ Yes
  ☐ No

5. Would you like to see the Anime Network in your area?
- ☐ Yes
- ☐ No

6. Would you pay $6.99/month for the Anime Network?
- ☐ Yes
- ☐ No

7. DEMAND YOUR ANIME! Yes, please sign me up for the Demand Your Anime Sweepstakes, with a chance to win a brand new Honda Civic Si and let my cable provider know that I'm interested in a 24/7 Anime channel!
- ☐ Yes
- ☐ No

8. What genre of manga and anime would you like to see from ADV?
(*Check all that apply*)
- ☐ adventure
- ☐ romance
- ☐ detective
- ☐ fighting
- ☐ horror
- ☐ sci-fi/fantasy
- ☐ sports

9. How many manga titles have you purchased in the last year?
- ☐ none
- ☐ 1-4
- ☐ 5-10
- ☐ 11+

10. Where do you make your manga purchases? (*Check all that apply*)
- ☐ comic store
- ☐ bookstore
- ☐ newsstand
- ☐ online
- ☐ other: _____
- ☐ department store
- ☐ grocery store
- ☐ video store
- ☐ video game store

11. What's your favorite anime-related website?
- ☐ advfilms.com
- ☐ anipike.com
- ☐ rightstuf.com
- ☐ animenewsservice.com
- ☐ animenewsnetwork.com
- ☐ animeondvd.com
- ☐ animenation.com
- ☐ animeonline.net
- ☐ planetanime.com
- ☐ other:

ENTRIES MUST BE RECEIVED BY DECEMBER 4, 2003

All information provided will be used for internal purposes only. We promise not to sell or otherwise divulge your information.